Lorenz on Leadership

Lessons on Effectively Leading People,
Teams, and Organizations

GENERAL STEPHEN R. LORENZ
USAF, RETIRED

Air University Press
Air Force Research Institute
Maxwell Air Force Base, Alabama

August 2012

Library of Congress Cataloging-in-Publication Data

Lorenz, Stephen R., 1951–
    Lorenz on leadership : lessons on effectively leading people, teams, and organizations / Stephen R. Lorenz.
      p. cm.
    ISBN 978-1-58566-222-7
    1. Lorenz, Stephen R., 1951– 2. Leadership—United States. 3. United States. Air Force—Anecdotes. 4. United States. Air Force—Management. 5. United States. Air Force—Military life. 6. Generals—United States—Biography—Anecdotes. 7. Conduct of life. I. Title.

    UB210.L67 2012
    658.4'092--dc23

                                 2012027598

Disclaimer

AIR FORCE RESEARCH INSTITUTE

Air University Press
Air Force Research Institute
155 N. Twining Street
Maxwell AFB, AL 36112-6026
http://aupress.au.af.mil

Dedicated to Leslie Ruth Layman Lorenz,
the love of my life and my Air Force teammate.

Contents

CONTENTS

Part 5

Other Articles

Foreword

If you want to learn about leadership, ask an experienced leader. Gen Stephen R. Lorenz, who retired as commander of Air Education and Training Command, has made the task accessible by giving us a collection of articles he wrote on the subject. General Lorenz started out like many graduates of the Air Force Academy with a heightened sense of leadership, one gleaned from watching and learning from leaders in classes, in the dorms, and on the parade grounds. Then, as now, he also had the opportunity to learn from a wide variety of important civilian and military leaders who visited the Academy.

Even as a lieutenant, General Lorenz developed a habitual practice of keeping a log of his activities in journals and scrapbooks. He thought about the styles of different leaders and found it satisfying to write about leadership at different points in his life, recognizing that the concept of leadership had different faces. He found that some practices are universally applicable, while some depend on the situation as well as the age and maturity of those being led. All this gave him insights into his own leadership style and fed his knowledge about the foundations of leadership.

As his writings on the subject grew into a sizeable collection over the years, General Lorenz not only found audiences that appreciated what he offered about leadership, but he began to see a set of standard principles that had useful effect in a wide range of conditions. Some examples that are well presented in this study include the point of "Balancing Shortfalls." It is a recognized principle that leaders never go to war with the resources they think they need—they must balance their shortfalls and show their staff and warriors that they can go forward anyway.

General Lorenz recognized that one of the toughest jobs commanders face is preparing their people to accept a new tasking. They have to find the resources to carry out the task, which means more work for everyone. Thus, while it is difficult to accept a new tasking because of the additional work involved, they find that people will work harder if the importance of the job is shared with the workers.

Many audiences found General Lorenz an engaging speaker. He commonly used popular subjects, even videos of Homer Simpson, to carry the message. Leaders must recognize the need to communicate to the sensitivities of their audience. He also reminds us to take our jobs, but not ourselves, seriously.

Nothing speaks better to the subject of effective leadership than the need to develop professionally. General Lorenz believes that leadership is tied to a continuing study of the profession, thus the need for leaders to read. He particularly advocates reading biographies of great leaders. He found that learning from other's experiences helped keep him from wasting time reinventing the wheel. And reading, like any other leadership development, is a lifetime experience because, as he describes it, "Life is a marathon, not a 50-yard dash."

John A. Shaud, PhD
General, USAF, Retired
Director, Air Force Research Institute

About the
Author

Gen Stephen R. Lorenz is a retired Air Force four-star general who currently serves as president and chief executive officer of the US Air Force Academy Endowment. His last military assignment was as the commander, Air Education and Training Command (AETC), Randolph AFB, Texas. He was responsible for the recruiting, training, and education of Air Force personnel. His command included the Air Force Recruiting Service, two numbered air forces, and Air University. AETC trains more than 340,000 students per year and consists of 12 bases, more than 88,000 active-duty, Reserve, Guard, civilians, and contractors, and 1,485 trainer, fighter, and mobility aircraft.

General Lorenz graduated from the Air Force Academy in 1973, and then attended undergraduate pilot training at Craig AFB, Alabama. He has commanded at every level, including an air refueling wing that won the 1994 Riverside Trophy for Best Wing in 15th Air Force, and an air mobility wing that won the 1995 Armstrong Trophy for Best Wing in 21st Air Force. He commanded the training wing at the Air Force Academy as the commandant of cadets. He also served as the deputy assistant secretary for budget, Office of the Assistant Secretary of the Air Force for Financial Management and Comptroller, Headquarters US Air Force, Washington, DC.

On 16 July 2010, he was awarded the Order of the Sword by the AETC Airmen. He is a command pilot with 3,600 hours in 10 aircraft.

Preface

Studying history and leadership has been my hobby for most of my life. I remember looking at illustrated histories of the American Civil War when I was seven or eight years old. Later when I was just 10, my father, who was an Air Force captain at the time, took me on a tour of the World War I battlefield at Verdun, France. I cannot remember when I was not reading or studying about all types of leaders—or visiting historical sites with my family and friends. Even today, my wife of 37 years, Leslie, jokes about all the battlefields she has visited with me by saying, "If you have seen one cannon on a battlefield, you have seen them all." Even our three children have walked the ground at numerous battlefields, including Gettysburg, Little Big Horn, Normandy—and yes, I took them to Verdun, France.

I started writing about leadership when I was a cadet, but really got started at Ellsworth AFB, South Dakota, in 1975. As a lieutenant working on my master's degree at the base education office, I was frustrated with our squadron leadership, and, through the eyes of a 24-year-old, I knew that I had all the answers. Fortunately, my lieutenant colonel squadron commander at the time was a wonderful mentor and extremely patient leader who spent time with me explaining that running a 150-person squadron was just a little bit more challenging than I might think.

Years later, when I was fortunate to command a similar Air Force squadron I realized how right he was. Over the years, I have worked for numerous great bosses who have continued to mentor me, and I learned just as much from many great peers and subordinates, including wonderful noncommissioned officers and civil servants. You see leaders come in all shapes and sizes, ranks, and professions. Leaders are everywhere if you know how and where to look.

Another hobby that I enjoy and that facilitates the study of leadership is visiting libraries and book stores. Over the years, I have noticed that very few Airmen take the time to write. There are normally numerous books about Soldiers, Sailors, Marines, and Coast Guardsmen and their great deeds. If you are lucky, you might find on the shelves a book full of airplane pictures. We do love our machines, but Airmen are just as accomplished as leaders as any other group.

The first article I wrote that was actually published in a base newspaper was "Lorenz on Leadership, Part I." This article was printed in the base paper at Castle AFB, California, in 1987. I do not know why

I wrote it in the middle of the night during an operational readiness inspection as we were generating aircraft to put on alert, but I did. This small step led me to continue to study leadership and build a briefing by the same name which I have given over 500 times in the last 25 years.

I have had a lot of help and feedback over the years in writing articles and building briefings. I want to thank my numerous executive officers, aides, commander's action group members, public affairs officers, judge advocate generals, and senior enlisted advisors for assisting me. They all helped improve the product.

I hope you enjoy these articles on leadership, but what I really hope is that as leaders you get inspired to write your own stories that will help mentor future generations of leaders. If I can do it, so can you!

PART 1

Articles from *Air and Space Power Journal*

Lorenz on Leadership, Part I

In 1987 I was commander of the 93rd Air Refueling Squadron at Castle AFB in Merced, California. Late one night, I sat down and wrote out a list of leadership principles. There was nothing magical about them—they were simply useful precepts I had learned over the years. Today, especially after the terrorist attacks of 11 September 2001, our leaders need to reflect on the principles that guide them. I do not seek to instill mine on the readers of this compilation. Rather, I only ask that Air Force leaders reflect on what their principles are, regardless of whether or not they have written them down. That said, I offer the following for consideration.

Balancing Shortfalls

Shortfalls occur in our professional and personal lives. We never seem to have enough time, money, or manpower. The essence of this "scarcity principle" lies in accepting the reality of limited resources and becoming adept at obtaining superior results in less-than-ideal situations. Equally important, once people acknowledge the scarcity of resources, they need not bemoan the situation any longer. In other words, they should "deal with it." Leaders must carry out the mission with the resources they have. They have to make it happen! This is part of being a military commander and leader. Commanders never go to war with all the resources they think they need—they balance their shortfalls to accomplish the mission.

Keeping Our Eyes on the Ball

In order to prevail, leaders must always keep in mind what they want to accomplish and not become distracted, regardless of the task. They must articulate the mission to their people. During my tenure as director of the Air Force budget, I didn't consider the budget the mission so much as I considered it a means for our service to defend the United States through the exploitation of air and space. In the Air

A version of this article was published as "Lorenz on Leadership," *Air and Space Power Journal* 19, no. 2 (Summer 2005): 5–9.

Force, this means that leaders must connect actions and troops to the mission and never lose sight of this important relationship.

Leaders can assure their people's well-being (a major ingredient of mission accomplishment) by knowing how they feel and how they are doing. They should look their people in the eye and ask how they are. Eyes don't lie; they reflect happiness, sadness, or stress. To get an honest answer, one should ask at least *three times* and do so more emphatically each time: "How are you doing?"

The first response is always, "Fine." The second, "I'm okay." Finally, when they realize that their leader is truly interested, they respond honestly. By the way, the only difference between a younger person and someone my age is the amount of scar tissue. Because I have lived longer than most of my military colleagues on active duty and therefore have more scar tissue, I can probably disguise my feelings more effectively. But the eyes are the true indicator. Again, leaders must never lose sight of the primary objective: to focus on the mission and take care of their people.

Those Who Do Their Homework Win

The equation for this principle is simple: knowledge = power. For example, take the battle for scarce resources. The person who has the most compelling story, backed by the strongest data, gets the most resources. We have seen this principle, which applies universally to all other undertakings, demonstrated repeatedly throughout history—especially military history!

The Toughest Word to Say in the English Language

According to an old adage, the most difficult word to say in English is *no*. But I have a contrarian's view. Saying *no* finishes the situation; saying *yes*, however, carries with it additional tasks, commitments, and responsibilities. For instance, when I agree to speak to a group, I have taken a more difficult path than I would have by declining. If I say *no* to a request for funding an initiative, my job is finished. If I say *yes*, then I must take on the task of finding resources. Leaders should also consider the effects of a response on working relationships. If a leader responds affirmatively 95 percent of the time, his or her people will readily accept the fact that the leader has carefully considered their request before responding negatively. I never say *no* until I research the issue and look into all of the alternatives. To this day, it still amazes me that most of the time I can say *yes* if I do a little work and make a personal commitment.

New Ideas Need Time and Nurturing to Grow and Bear Fruit

In order to overcome some of the challenges we face today, we need people to think and act out of the box. Furthermore, we must have the patience and faith to stay the course. Things do not happen overnight; people have to work very hard to make things happen. They must sell their ideas and do their homework without concern for who gets the credit. This principle is very important to remember as new generations of Airmen enter the Air Force to help fight the global war on terrorism.

Leaders Should Not Lose Their Temper—Unless They Plan To

To navigate the necessary course of action and ensure mission accomplishment, a leader must be willing to use more than one approach. Earlier in my career, I saw my boss—a mild-mannered, consummately professional four-star general—storm into a meeting and angrily bark out criticisms to his senior staff. When we left the room, he looked at me, winked, and said that a person has to put across a different face in order for people to take him or her seriously. My boss had planned the whole incident. He had not lost his temper at all—he did it for effect. If leaders cannot control themselves, how can they control others? They must have self-discipline. They should never, ever lose their temper—unless they plan to.

All Decisions Should Pass the Sunshine Test

Because leaders must make difficult decisions every day, it's important for people in the trenches to know that the process is fair and above reproach. Toward that end, we must be as open and accessible as possible and always act as if our decisions were public knowledge—as if they appeared in the newspaper, for example. If leaders are forthright about why they made a decision, their people might disagree, but they will understand the underlying logic and continue to trust them. As Air Force leaders, we need only look to our service's core values—integrity first, service before self, and excellence in all we do—to arrive at solid decisions that gain the public trust and instill faith in our processes.

Ego: Both a Facilitator and a Detriment

A unit's success depends upon its members keeping their egos in check. We cannot afford to let them run amuck. We need confident, capable people who work together to enhance the organization rather than individuals who pursue their own selfish agendas. As my father taught me, leaders need people with ambition—not ambitious people. Early in my career, I applied for a development program—the predecessor of the current Air Force Intern Program. I had confidence that I would be accepted, so not seeing my name on the list came as a shock. To make matters worse, another officer in my squadron did make the cut.

Inwardly, I withdrew from the organization and walked around several days feeling hurt and angry. Eventually, though, I realized that the Air Force only owed me the opportunity to compete. On the day the board met, my records did not meet its standards. Whose fault was that? Mine—no one else's. I put the issue behind me and embraced my squadron mate. This experience taught me the negative effect of allowing my ego to dominate my actions—specifically, my failure to realize that the Air Force had not promised to select me for the program. It did, however, guarantee me equitable consideration and fair competition. I should have expected nothing else. An Air Force person should compete only with himself or herself, striving for improvement every day!

Work the Boss's Boss's Problems

This principle goes one step beyond the adage "work your boss's problems." Most people make a decision through a soda straw, but if they would rise up two levels above themselves, they could open the aperture of that straw and get a strategic view of the decision. Taking a "God's-eye" view—looking through the eyes of their boss's boss—allows them to make a much better decision. That is, leaders must become deeply committed to the organization and make their boss's challenges their own. If they can achieve this type of commitment—regardless of who the boss is or which political party controls the government—the only thing that matters is enhancing mission accomplishment by making the best decisions possible and doing the right thing under the circumstances.

Self-Confidence and Motivation: Keys to Any Great Endeavor

We can attribute most successful endeavors to persevering and putting forth maximum effort. Whenever I speak about leadership, I always begin with a quotation from Sir Winston Churchill: "To every man there comes in his lifetime that special moment when he is figuratively tapped on the shoulder and offered that chance to do a very special thing, unique to him and fitted to his talents. What a tragedy if that moment finds him unprepared or unqualified for that which would be his finest hour."

I am particularly attracted to this statement because of the great things Churchill accomplished, even though he faced failure and defeat many times. Regardless of the difficulty or hardship, he remained committed and motivated and never gave up. Churchill's words represent a call to action that has helped me overcome such challenges as surviving engineering courses as a cadet as well as serving as a wing commander, commandant of cadets at the Air Force Academy, and budget director for the Air Force despite having no prior experience in budgetary matters. Although I lacked in-depth knowledge of budget and finance, perseverance got me through, as always. I never gave up. My best advice? Never give up. Never, ever give up!

Apply Overwhelming Combat Power to the Point That Will Have the Most Effect

I have a simple organizational method that has served me well for many years. I like to approach issues, goals, and tasks—"big to small, top to bottom, or left to right." That is, I believe that one must be able to see the entire forest before working on individual trees. We must understand the big-picture issues before delving into smaller details. From a broad point of view, I find it helpful to pursue goals by progressing from the short term through the midterm to the long term. Leaders should make sure their subordinates have not only the "overall road map" they need for direction, but also the resources to plan and complete tasks.

One of my favorite and most beneficial experiences involved an aircraft-sanitation worker at McGuire AFB, New Jersey. During a customer-focus class that I taught in an effort to counter what I perceived as lackadaisical attitudes prevalent in the organization, I noticed a lady in the audience whose body language was so agitated that she was figuratively *screaming* at me. I stopped the class and asked her what was wrong. Jeanie said she was frustrated because no one would help her with a work problem. I told her that if she explained the situation to me, I would try to help.

According to Jeanie, the sanitation truck that she operated was designed for servicing a KC-10, which sits high off the ground. Normally, she hooked the truck's waste-removal hose to the aircraft, flipped a switch, and gravity pulled the contents into her vehicle. At that time, however, McGuire also had the C-141, which sits only three feet off the ground. Consequently, when she attempted the same procedure on the C-141, the hose bent because it was not fully extended, as with the KC-10, and became clogged with waste. She then had to disconnect the hose, lift it over her head, and shake it to clear the obstruction—clearly an unpleasant task that she had to repeat multiple times if the aircraft's lavatory was completely full.

Although such a problem might seem trivial, on a large aircraft that makes extended flights, the lavatory is a mission-essential piece of equipment. Armed with the knowledge of Jeanie's problem, I organized a team to solve it, and the team members did so by engineering and installing a 3.2-horsepower engine that proved more than capable of overcoming the clearance problem. But the greatest accomplishment in this case was neither the technical solution nor the vastly improved sanitation procedure but the effect the process had on Jeanie. It revived and energized her. Thereafter, each time I saw Jeanie she proudly displayed her truck, which she had polished and shined so highly that it would likely meet a hospital's sanitation standards. This story drives home the point that leaders must look for both verbal and nonverbal messages from the people in their organization. If they can reach the person who operates the sanitation truck, then they can reach anyone.

Study the Profession and Read—Especially Biographies

During our Air Force careers, we have many opportunities to add to our education and knowledge. America's future depends upon our maximizing and complementing these occasions with our own regimen of reading and development. As a lifetime student of leadership, I have an insatiable appetite for learning and regularly read two or three books at a time. I have dedicated myself to learning from other people's experiences so that I do not waste time trying to reinvent the wheel. Studying and learning how other leaders overcame adversity will build confidence in one's own ability to make tough decisions. I have found my study of Gen Colin Powell and Gen Henry "Hap" Arnold especially rewarding.

Take Your Job (Not Yourself) Seriously

To drive home the important concepts when I discuss leadership, I include comical—sometimes outrageous—videos and pictures to accompany each principle. Audiences seem both surprised and refreshed to see a general officer use David Letterman-style "top-10 lists" and irreverent videos ranging from Homer Simpson to bizarre advertisements as part of a serious presentation. However, I see these methods as the ideal way of delivering my message. Leaders must realize that because they communicate with a diverse, cross-generational population, they need to speak in terms their audience will understand.

A leader must create a common, shared vision that everyone can comprehend and accept. I like to try to communicate my vision by talking about an experience or using an analogy that everyone can relate to, understand, and remember. It is critical that leaders deliver their message in easily grasped terminology. They should employ a type of universal device akin to the "Romulan translator" depicted in the *Star Trek* television series. The medium used by the communicator can take the form of an analogy, a video, or a story. However, the critical point is that the communicator packages and delivers the message in a format that the varied groups we lead today will understand.

Today's leaders were born primarily during the last half of the twentieth century. They could have been born 100 years earlier or 100 years from now. Most, but not all, American leaders were born in the United States. They could have been born in another country like Iraq or Cambodia, but the majority was born in America. The United States, whether it wants to be or not, is the world's greatest power, and air and space power is now the permanent instrument of that power.

Every one of the current leaders in our military at some time made a conscious decision to become a defender, not a defended. Balancing this all together, we see that our leaders have a heavy burden leading others in the global war on terrorism. Every day they get up in the morning to lead, and they have to give it their very best—not their second best. Visiting the wounded Soldiers, Sailors, Marines, and Airmen in our hospitals makes us realize that leaders owe their people the very best. They cannot afford to have a bad day! They must know who they are and how they lead; they must have their own list of leadership principles.

As I said before, the most important point about these 13 personal leadership principles that I have laid out is to encourage leaders to define their own principles. I have sought to motivate and aid our service's leaders in identifying and clarifying their positions—not in memorizing mine. In order for a leader's set of principles to be effective, they should be based on a foundation—such as the ideals embodied in the Air Force's core values—and they must reflect who that leader is! It is never too early or too late to write down a set of personal leadership principles. Future leaders in today's Air Force should start now—they will never regret it, and it will make them better leaders for our nation.

Lorenz on Leadership, Part II

In the summer of 2005, when I was director of financial management and comptroller at the Pentagon, *Air and Space Power Journal* published an article of mine titled "Lorenz on Leadership." Later, as the commander of Air University (AU), I sat down to proffer some additional thoughts on my favorite subject: leadership. I hope that you share my enthusiasm for the study of leadership!

Never, Ever Give Up

In my last article, I quoted Winston Churchill and briefly explained why I find him so fascinating. One of his most famous quotations was "never, ever, ever give up!" Churchill was a man who met failure face-to-face many times in his life. He ran for parliament and lost, only to be elected two years later. When he was the first sea lord of the Admiralty (equivalent to the US secretary of the Navy), he planned the Gallipoli campaign in Turkey, which turned out to be an abject failure, and was fired. During the early 1930s, he railed against Nazi tyranny, but nobody listened to him. Then in 1940 he became the prime minister who led England in the war against Hitler. After the defeat of Germany but before the war against Japan ended, the people held an election, throwing him and his party out of office! Five years later, in 1950 he became prime minister for a second time. Wow! Talk about perseverance, tenacity, and strength of character! I admire Churchill so much because the story of how he overcame his struggles in life is an example for all of us to follow.

As a graduate of the Air Force Academy—and I can truly say that those four years were tough—I could handle the physical, military, and mental aspects without much difficulty; however, my struggles were mostly academic. You see, I was on the dean's "other" list six of eight semesters. I enjoyed courses in aeronautical engineering, computer science, and electrical engineering so much that I took them twice. Although this may seem humorous today, it is not an aspect of my history that I am particularly proud of; nevertheless, the lesson here is that one must never, ever give up. While many of my friends

A version of this article was published as "Lorenz on Leadership: Part 2," *Air and Space Power Journal* 22, no. 1 (Spring 2008): 9–13.

were going out to enjoy themselves on the weekends, I forced myself to concentrate on my studies, especially those math and science courses that held little interest for me—the ones I had to work on twice as hard just to pass. This particular aspect of character served me well in the more than 37 years I served in the Air Force. As the commander of AU, I was lucky enough to be responsible for most of the education in the entire US Air Force. Isn't America a great country?

Life Is a Marathon, Not a 50-Yard Dash

We've all seen examples of athletes or teams that, in a moment of almost certain glory, celebrated too early, only to see victory swept from their grasp by an opponent who, not surprisingly, never, ever gave up. In our lives, it is important to remember that we must prepare to run a marathon—not a 50-yard dash. I'm sure that in your careers, you've seen military members start a task in a sprint only to find out it required marathon-like stamina. Their first inclination was to give up because it was too hard. They didn't do their homework, so they spent all their energy in the early stages and couldn't complete the task. You see, life is about training and being prepared for opportunities when they come—you don't train for a marathon in the same way you train for a 50-yard dash! You must invest time and effort in understanding your goals and then in charting a course to accomplish them. I used the short-, mid-, and long-term approach, and I taught my people this as well. There's a lot of truth to the cliché "What's the best way to eat an elephant? One bite at a time." Understand the mission; do your homework; and never, ever give up!

Never Develop a Sense of Entitlement

You will never get what you want when you think you deserve it. Rewards always come later than we are typically willing to accept. Since we are human, we frequently compare ourselves to our peers, but we should really compete only with ourselves—not others. We see others being rewarded, so we take an "I should have won that" or "I deserved that" attitude. If you get the feeling that "you deserve" something or feel that the organization "owes you," immediately stop what you're doing, take a deep breath, and reevaluate yourself because once you go down that path of "me, me, me," it's hard to turn around. Over the course of my career in the Air Force, I saw a number of people develop an entitlement attitude, only to end up disappointed and bitter. When this happens, the person loses, his or her family loses, and ultimately the organization loses. The Air Force or any job owes you only one thing—the opportunity to compete and serve!

As a Leader, You Must Reach the Acceptance Phase of Grief Faster Than the People You Lead

There are five traditional stages of grief: denial, anger, bargaining, depression, and acceptance. When a challenge arises in your organization, it is important that, as a leader, you reach the final stage long before your people do. In 1993 I took command of the 22nd Air Refueling Wing at March AFB, California. A few weeks after taking command, we had an operational readiness inspection (ORI), and the Airmen performed brilliantly! I was so proud. On the last day, we all gathered in the base theater for the outbrief. Horns, bells, and whistles were going off, and everyone was pumped about getting the ORI grade because they had worked so hard to do a great job. The inspector general (IG) took the stage, and in the first of four categories, we got a "high satisfactory," and in the second category, we got a "high satisfactory." As the briefing progressed, the noise level got lower and lower because everyone knew what was coming. That's right, an overall "high satisfactory"—which really just means a "satisfactory."

The IG then got up and left, leaving me, the wing commander, in this room with these tremendous people who had done a wonderful job, but it felt like all the oxygen had been absolutely sucked out of the place. You could have heard a pin drop. Now, as the leader, what was I to do? I had five options: denial, anger, bargaining, depression, and acceptance. I thought long and hard about what to say, and having reached acceptance faster than the folks in the room, I came up with the following: "The IG is a great group of individuals who have come here with a difficult task, and we are all better off because of their feedback. But I'll tell you what I think. I think that grade is the biggest bunch of 'BS' I've ever heard of."

At first there was no reaction to my remarks, but then the entire room erupted in shouts and cheers! All I had done was reach acceptance of our final grade and then put into words what everyone else in the room was thinking. However, imagine my surprise when we all went to the club to celebrate the end of the ORI and saw that a video-tape of me making my statement about the grade was on a permanent television loop for everyone to see and hear, over and over again! As a leader, you must get through all the stages of grief before your people do, so you can *lead* them through the tough times.

It's Not about *You*!

The sooner you can wrap your mind around this one, the sooner you can focus on what's right and get out of your own way. Leadership is not about you; it's about the organization and the people who work in it. As a leader, you set the tone of the organization and give your folks the tools to succeed; then you must get out of the way and let them do their jobs! Let's take a lesson from sports. Professional football teams have coaches—folks who devise the strategies and the plays. They look at the team's talent and put the right players in the right position for the best possible outcome, but they are not out there running the ball—their players do that.

As a leader, it's your job to put the right folks in the right places to ensure mission success. I've seen too many leaders who were afraid to trust in their subordinates and the organization; consequently, the pride and attitude of the workers suffered. Leadership is not about: "Hey, look at me. I'm the leader. Look at what *my* organization has done." Those who pursue the awards, promotions, and accolades are often the ones exposed in time and eventually fall by the wayside. People see right through someone who has his or her own agenda, and that person's ability to lead is immediately sacrificed. Leaders have to understand that it is about the people, the organization, and the mission.

A few years ago, my spouse reminded me that it is indeed not about me. We were at a conference, and during the course of the meeting, I was asked a certain question several times. I don't recall the question, and it's not important. But I do remember being asked this question for what seemed like a dozen times, so to be quite honest, I was tired of hearing and answering it. While we were seated at dinner that night, a young cadet happened to ask the very same question again, and without hesitation I gave him a halfhearted, emotionless answer. My mannerisms reflected my frustration with the question, and my answer simply vocalized it.

Overhearing what I had said, my spouse squeezed my arm and said, "Honey, I know you've heard that question a dozen times, but that's the first time that cadet has ever asked it." She was absolutely right. The cadet didn't know how many times I had been asked that question, nor did he care. He only knew that he had asked it and wanted an answer. I immediately sought him out and gave him the right answer with the right attitude. Remember, it's not about you! (Postscript: this also applies to every promotion ceremony, parade, and speech you will ever attend or participate in. You must be enthusiastic and sincere, no matter how many times you have done it before!)

You Want People with Ambition Working for You, Not Ambitious People

My father taught me this statement a long time ago. As a leader, you want people with ambition working for you—those are the folks who are goal oriented and possess a willingness to strive for excellence. They are the ones who are willing to do what it takes to fulfill the mission, whether it's staying late or working harder to ensure that the goals and mission of the organization are complete. On the other hand, ambitious people often have an ulterior motive behind their actions—motives shrouded in "what's in it for me?" versus "what's good for the organization?" As a leader, you will have to know the difference.

You Never Know When You Are Going to Make a Difference

In 1996 I became commandant of cadets at the Air Force Academy. In my first two years, nine cadets died due to rock-climbing, car and aircraft accidents, and one to pulmonary edema at high altitude. She was a third-class cadet (a sophomore)—a 19-year-old who was as sharp as a tack! At the memorial service in the Cadet Chapel, I steeled myself to go talk to her mother and father.

What could I say? This family had given their national treasure to the Air Force, and she dies during training. In this moment, how could I attempt to assuage her parents' grief? I walked up and introduced myself to her mother. "Ma'am," I said, "My name is Steve Lorenz." She immediately stopped me and said, "I know who you are, General Lorenz; my daughter told me about you. She had just earned her superintendent's pin for getting good grades, and you saw her on the terrazzo where all the cadets formed up and congratulated her for doing a great job. She immediately went back to her room and called us to say, 'The commandant of cadets told me how proud he was of me for earning the superintendent's pin.'" This conversation with the mother is especially poignant to me because I do not remember talking to this young cadet at all, but this is what the mother remembered. In a few seconds, I had made a difference in someone's life. You truly never know when you are going to make a difference.

During my tenure on the Joint Staff, I worked several layers below the man I consider one of the greatest military officers of our time, Gen Colin Powell. Now, before the days of e-mail, we used to hand carry correspondence into his office. I distinctly remember going to his executive officer's desk one day to deliver a staff package. As I turned to leave, a major entered the room with his grandmother and said, "Grandmother, there is General Powell's office." At that precise moment, General Powell came out of his office to retrieve a package. Seeing the major wearing his Joint Staff badge and his guest, he asked, "Major, is this your grandmother?" The major said, "Yes," and then I saw General Powell gingerly take this lady's hand and for the next couple of minutes tell the grandmother what a great job her grandson was doing and how without his support he would be unable to do his job. General Powell then reached into a desk drawer, presented the grandmother with a Joint Staff pin, and said he was off to a meeting, but he thanked her again for allowing her grandson to serve. As soon as his door closed, I turned to look at the grandmother, and you could certainly see that her heart was aflutter—and so was mine. You see, in less than a minute, General Powell had made a difference in her life, the major's life, and my life. It takes only a moment to make a difference, and you may never know when that moment will present itself.

Being in Our Profession Is All about Service to Others

I am reminded of the photograph of the chief master sergeant stationed in Iraq who, after working a full 12-hour shift, would go to the inpatient ward and hold a wounded Iraqi child who had lost her entire family. To me, this is what being in the military is all about—service. Harking back to the days when civilians referred to someone who joined the military, oftentimes they didn't say that "he joined the Air Force," or "he joined the Army." Instead they said, "He joined the service." Why? Because that's what we're all about—service to others. I imagine that after his long shift, the good chief just wanted to go back to his tent and unwind, but he had made a commitment to make a difference and was prepared to execute that duty, no matter the cost. This is a lesson we can all use. When we raise our right hands to take the oath or when we put on our uniforms, we are saying "I want to serve" and "send me, I'll go." There is no distinction between being in the military and serving—they are one and the same.

What Will Your Leadership Legacy Be?

In my office, I have a quotation framed and positioned on my desk where I can see it every day. It says, "My biggest fear is that I will look back on my life and wonder what I did with it." Sooner or later, it will be time for all of us to hang up our uniforms and find something else to do. As I look back over my career, I continually wonder if I did enough—if I did all that I could to make a difference and be a positive influence on others. Hopefully I did.

I was lucky enough to travel with the chief of staff to Balad, Iraq. We visited the hospital there, and one of the many individuals I talked to was an Army lieutenant colonel—a tall, thin, lean, and gaunt man with dark circles under his eyes. He was very tired! He was a battalion commander who had been in the country for 11 months and was visiting one of his wounded troops. After chatting for a few minutes, I backed away from him to the other side of the tent, and people began to flow between us. As I stood there watching him, I said to myself, "You know, Lorenz, you've been a commander several times in the last 35 years. I just hope you are a good-enough leader to lead someone like that." You see, you must never, ever stop trying to be the best leader you can be.

Lorenz on Leadership, Part III

In 1987 I first wrote out my thoughts on leadership. The compilation included 13 principles that AU published in the summer of 2005 as part I in what became the "Lorenz on Leadership" series. Later, in the spring of 2008, AU published part II, which included an additional eight leadership principles. Over the last few years, various experiences have highlighted yet another group of principles that I present for your consideration.

When I first wrote down these principles, I certainly didn't intend to prescribe an approved way to think or lead. After all, none of these principles is unique. I took them from other leaders who influenced me through the years, hoping that readers would develop their own set of principles.

This Is a Family Business

Families are important—this goes without saying. When I say that this is a "family business," realize that the term *family* encompasses more than just your immediate loved ones. In this case, it also includes our extended Air Force family. I can't tell you the countless times I've heard people thank their "brothers and sisters in the Air Force family." Sometimes they do so at promotion or retirement ceremonies, but I've also heard the phrase at going-away parties and in daily conversations.

When we take time to reflect, we recognize the bond we share with others in the Air Force is stronger than that for most coworkers in the business world. This is especially true when we factor in the ties we create after remote tours, overseas assignments, and long combat deployments. You see, the term *brothers and sisters in arms* is no accident. As we live, train, sweat, and bleed together, these bonds grow so strong that the only language we have to describe our feelings for each other is the language of family—the Air Force family.

Building a strong Air Force family means that all of us share a commitment to our fellow Airmen, treating them in ways that reflect our commitment. We should all live in a way that maximizes our ability to

A version of this article was published as "Lorenz on Leadership: Part 3," *Air and Space Power Journal* 24, no. 3 (Fall 2010): 5–12.

touch the lives of others. This means that we should have a healthy focus on others, not on ourselves. Paraphrasing a wise person, we should not think less of ourselves; we should think of ourselves less.

Now, I would most certainly be remiss if I didn't specifically mention our spouses—our foundation. These are the men and women who keep us strong, help us through the tears, and enable each of us to serve in the world's greatest Air Force. Our lives need balance, and our spouses help provide that stability. I like to use the analogy that such balance is similar to the spokes of a bicycle wheel. You see, a bicycle needs balanced spokes in order to provide a smooth ride. Our lives are no different. I think of the spokes as the different priorities in our lives. If one of the spokes—like the relationship with your spouse, the needs of your children, or the responsibilities at work—gets slighted, the wheel no longer rolls the way it should. It might even stop rolling all together.

We must balance the spokes in our lives very deliberately and carefully. When we are balancing shortfalls and managing a limited amount of time, money, and manpower, our spouses are often shortchanged. We can't afford to let that happen; we must always make time to tell our spouses how much we appreciate them. It only takes a minute to let them know how much we care. Maintaining the friendship, trust, and energy in a relationship is a full-time job. It's up to you to make it a fun job—for both you and your spouse.

Successful Teams Are Built on Trust

Although the Air Force family helps support and steer us through our service, trust is the foundation of our existence. This trust is a two-way street—both within our service and with the American public. When an Airman from security forces tells me that the base is secure, I know without a doubt that all is safe. Before flying, I always review the forms documenting maintenance actions on that aircraft. The aircraft maintainer's signature at the bottom of the forms is all I need to see to have complete confidence in the safety of that airplane. I liken it to the cell phone commercial many of you have probably seen. Although there may be a single man or woman in front, he or she speaks with the voice of thousands standing behind. A successful team is one that works together, enabled and empowered by trust.

On our Air Force team, everyone's ability to perform his or her function is what builds trust and makes the machine run so smoothly. Ultimately, we all share the same goal—the defense of our nation and its ideals. That's the common denominator, regardless of rank, where trust and mutual respect are paramount. At every base, in every shop and office, Air Force leadership (officer, enlisted, and civilian) consistently sets the example. We are all role models and always on the job. Our Airmen live up to these expectations every day.

The trust and faith we share with the American public are a different story. There are constantly under scrutiny—and for good reason. Members of the American public "trust" us with their sons and daughters—and billions of dollars of their hard-earned money. That trust is built upon a foundation of accountability. To be accountable is to be subject to the consequences of our choices. Whether we choose to do the right thing—to act with integrity, service, and excellence—or not, we have to be prepared to accept the consequences.

We are accountable for the choices we make in our personal lives. The vast majority of choices that get people in trouble involve alcohol, sex, drugs, and/or money. Each year, some of us make wrong choices in these areas and are held accountable. If you know Airmen who are headed down a wrong path, help them before they make a bad choice.

We are also accountable for the choices we make as military professionals. We must adhere to the standards we learned from our first days in uniform. When Airmen cut corners by failing to follow tech order guidance or by violating a flying directive, we must hold them accountable. We must police each other because if we don't, small lapses will lead to bigger ones, and the entire Air Force family will eventually suffer. Overlooking a lapse is the same as condoning it.

When you assume responsibility for others as a supervisor or commander, it is important to realize that you've taken a big leap in accountability. Simply put, you are accountable for the choices your people make. That is why you must lead by example. Your people need to see that you set high standards and live according to those standards. You must also enforce standards within your unit. You should correct deficiencies at the lowest level before they grow into something bigger. Remember this—units with high standards have high morale. It's been that way throughout military history.

Feedback Fuels Change

Trust and accountability rely on feedback for success. We all have blind spots—areas where we think things are better than they are. To correct these, we need to be aware of them. This means that we need to encourage dissenting opinions and negative feedback. We should ask open-ended questions: What are we missing? How can we do this better? What's the downside? What will other people say?

When our people answer, we must welcome their inputs, even when those inputs don't cast our leadership in the best light. In the end, our time as leaders will be judged by the quality of our decisions and the accomplishments of our people. The personal price we pay in the short term for creating candor in our organizations is well worth the long-term professional and institutional benefits of hearing the best ideas and eradicating our blind spots.

In order to encourage our people to voice their alternative ideas and criticisms, we have to be confident enough in our people to listen to negative feedback and dissenting opinions, find the best way forward, and then lead in a positive direction. We all like the "warm fuzzies" we get when people agree with our ideas and give us positive feedback. We naturally dislike the "cold pricklies" that come when people disagree with us and point out our shortcomings. As leaders, we have to be mature enough to deal with negative feedback without punishing the source; the best leaders encourage frank feedback, especially when it is negative.

As followers, we must work at creating candor as well. While the leader must set the tone for open communication, it is important that those of us who voice dissenting opinions or give negative feedback do so in a way that it can have the most effect. We can't expect our leaders to be superhuman—this means we should speak in a way that doesn't turn them off immediately.

We should also remember that the leader is ultimately responsible for the direction of the organization. If he or she decides to do something that you disagree with, voice your opinion—but be ready to accept the leader's decision. As long as the boss's decision isn't illegal or immoral, you should carry it out as though the idea was your own. That's the mark of a professional Airman.

All Visions Require Resourcing

As leaders, we must be prepared to face many kinds of potential challenges, both anticipated and unexpected. While working on the challenge, as a leader, you will be faced with balancing a limited amount of time, money, and manpower. In order to optimally allocate these critical resources, leaders must develop visions for their organization.

To realize a vision, several things need to happen. First, you must align the vision with one of our core service functions. The closer to the core, the easier it will be to gain support and, eventually, resourcing. Next, take the vision and develop a strategy. Depending on your vision, the strategy may involve acquisition, implementation, execution, modification, or one of many other aspects. Let your strategy start at the 40 percent solution, then evolve to 80 percent, and finally to 98 percent. Realize the process is continual and that you will never get to 100 percent.

With the strategy in place, you can start socializing the vision. Socialization will also help your vision progress and grow roots through increased organizational support and understanding. The support will help you champion the concept for resourcing. After all, your vision must have resourcing in order to come true. Those resources will go to winners, not to losers, so invest the time and energy to be a winner.

In life, and especially in the Air Force, priorities and personnel are always changing. Over time, your vision will need to adapt to the realities of change. It will require even greater persistence and objectivity. Giving your vision roots and aligning it with core functions will create something that can be handed off and sustained through change. The best ideas, sustained by hard work, can be carried forward by any leader.

You may also find yourself joining an organization and accepting someone else's vision. In this situation, evaluate their vision against current realities and resourcing priorities. If they've done their homework, the project will be easy to move forward. If they haven't, assess the vision to determine if it should move ahead or if its time has passed.

Objective Leaders Are Effective Leaders

In essence, a leader develops a vision to help guide decision making. Most decisions are made without much thought—almost instinctively based on years of experience. Other decisions, however, involve time and thought, and they can impact other people. These are the decisions where the process is an art; it defines who we are as leaders.

Saying this isn't a stretch. As leaders, we do things in order to create a desired effect. Making the "best" decision hits at the core of creating that effect and, in turn, is an essential aspect of being an effective leader. Now, these aren't decisions that involve "right versus wrong"—or lying, cheating, or stealing—we must never compromise our integrity. In fact, most of these decisions involve "right versus right," and the decision may be different today than it was yesterday. This is what can make them so challenging. Let's take a moment to look at the elements involved in making the "best" decision.

Effective decisions require objectivity. The old adage "the more objective you are, the more effective you are" has never been more accurate or applicable than it is today. It can be tempting to look at decisions through the lens of a small straw. Effective leaders must step back and gain a much broader view; they must open their aperture. I've always advocated looking at issues and decisions from the viewpoint of your boss's boss. This approach helps to open the aperture and maintain objectivity.

In order to gain the broad, objective view, leaders must work to gather a complete picture of the situation. Some call this situational awareness; others call it a 360-degree view of the issue. In either case, that awareness involves considering all of the variables that weigh into the decision, the interests involved in the decision, and the potential consequences of the decision. The potential consequences must include possible second- and third-order consequences. Tough calls like these can involve individuals, organizations, and issues beyond those initially considered. Weigh the consequences against unit missions and organizational goals. Investigate how the decision will move things forward in the near, mid, and long term. This will provide the context for the decision and, although it will involve a lot of work, will result in the broadest view of the entire process.

Tough decisions can be very emotional. Don't let emotion play into the decision-making process. Emotion only serves to cloud the issue; it can potentially result in a decision where near-term happiness fades quickly into mid- and long-term unintended challenges. Leaders must look at decisions from the outside, unattached to the emotional influence from within. They must rise above such distractions in order to maintain their objectivity and keep their organizations headed in the "best" direction.

Train Wrecks—How Can We Prepare for Impending Crisis?

Unfortunately, it is the unanticipated crisis that often derails organizations headed in a positive direction. I like to call those unanticipated challenges "train whistles in the distance." In reality, it's pretty easy to know when trains are coming down the tracks. They are big, make lots of noise, and are accompanied by warning lights and bells. Trains typically run on a schedule, making it even easier to know when to either step to the side or hop onboard.

We rarely get the same notification from an impending crisis in the workplace. More often, it appears, seemingly from out of thin air, and immediately consumes more time than we have to give. Through frustrated, tired eyes, we wonder where the crisis came from in the first place. Even though we vow never to let it happen again, deep down we know that it's only a matter of time before the next one hits our organization by surprise.

Such an outlook is what helped create an entire school of thought called "crisis management." We have crisis action teams and emergency response checklists—we even build entire plans describing how to effectively deal with the train that we never saw coming. These impacts can be hard to absorb and usually leave "casualties" behind. Wouldn't it be better to prepare for specific contingencies and not rely on generic crisis-response checklists? Wouldn't it be better for the organization if a leader knew about the train long before it arrived?

So, how does a leader get the schedule for inbound trains? In many cases, just getting out of the office and talking to members of an organization can help a leader identify potential issues and areas of risk. By the same token, if you are a member of an organization and know of an upcoming challenge, it is your responsibility to research and report it.

Candor and objectivity alone will probably help catch 90 percent of the issues before they impact an organization. In order to achieve

100 percent, a leader must work hard to avoid complacency. When things get "quiet" within an organization, it doesn't necessarily mean that everything is being handled successfully. In fact, the hair on the back of every leader's neck should start to stand up when things get quiet. After all, it probably means that the leader isn't involved enough in the daily operation of the unit and that the first two elements, candor and objectivity, are being overlooked. This is the time to be even more aggressive about candor, information flow, and objectivity.

Leaders who work hard to enable candor, remain objective, and discourage complacency have a unique opportunity to steer their organizations in the best direction when challenges or crises loom. As they identify the inbound trains, leaders can decide whether to maneuver clear or to hop onboard. You see, each inbound train is an opportunity. It is a chance to fight for new resources—money and/or manpower—and to unify their team toward a common objective. Leaders should anticipate inbound trains as a means to improve their organizations.

So then, what is the best way for a leader to guide people through change? There are certainly many methods to do so, and each one depends on the type of change expected. In all cases, however, the principles that underlie the preparation for change are the same. Preparation builds confidence, helps a leader's organization be less fearful of approaching uncertainty, and ensures that the organization is much more effective once change arrives.

This is where education and training come into play. We educate in order to prepare for uncertainty. Education helps us understand why the change is necessary. It also helps us objectively assess the environment and rationale necessitating the change. With objectivity, we can unemotionally assess the benefits and drawbacks of the different potential courses of action. Education is a never-ending self-improvement process. The different levels occur at specific spots in our careers—opening doors and creating opportunities. Because the Air Force lines up education programs with future levels of responsibility, it can be difficult to adequately catch up on education. Never pass up the opportunity to further your education.

While education helps us prepare for uncertainty, training programs are designed to prepare for certainty. After all, it's those things we expect that fill our syllabi and lesson books. We train for them over and over until recognizing and reacting to them are second nature. This is one reason why we use checklists so much in the Air Force. They help lead us accurately through challenging times.

Through experience, our collective list of "certainty" grows. It shapes the evolution of our training programs. You see, when we react to a challenge, we create a certain result. Positive results reinforce the action and make us more confident. Although the positive result "trains" us to use the same response next time, it typically doesn't teach us to handle anything other than the exact same challenge. When we make mistakes or experience negative results, we have an opportunity to learn. Even though it may not be as much fun to investigate our failures, we are more apt to critically assess the challenge and develop other, more successful, potential courses of action.

As a leader, you must ensure your people have the education necessary to prepare them for uncertainty and the training to guide them through certainty. As an individual, you must aggressively pursue these opportunities to further develop yourself as well. Such preparation will instill the confidence necessary to embrace change.

In the End, People Are Still People

Although leadership will always be about the people we lead, technology has changed the way we do our jobs. Beyond the most noticeable and tangible aspects like e-mail, PowerPoint, and cell phones, technology has transformed the workplace in three main areas: collaboration, automation, and personal accessibility. Collaboration includes our ability to network, collect, and share information. Getting the right information to the right people when they need it isn't always as easy as it sounds. After all, accurate information is a key element in making objective decisions, and objectivity is what keeps our organizations headed in the best direction. Today's challenge, however, is managing the sheer volume of available information. Technological advancements will only make this challenge greater in years to come.

By automation, I'm talking about technology's impact on the tasks we do each and every day. Historically, automation has been one of the enablers for doing "more with less." Our most expensive asset is our people. Technology gives us the ability to energize certain efficiencies by replacing manpower with technology. Maintaining the balance of technology and manpower will continue to be a daily leadership challenge.

Lastly, accessibility applies to our ability to contact anyone, any-where, and anytime through voice and data communication. There are two key aspects of accessibility: how leaders make themselves available to others and how you, as a leader, take advantage of the availability of others. It is important that commanders, while mak-ing themselves available at all hours of the day, don't foster an envi-ronment where subordinates are afraid to get decisions from any-where but the top. At the same time, leaders must guard against exploiting the availability of others, especially subordinates. Such exploitation will only reinforce to subordinates that decisions can only come from the top.

Accessibility has also changed how we make ourselves available to others. Many commanders like to say that they have an "open door policy." Don't fool yourself into thinking that issues will always walk through the open door. Leaders still need to escape the electronic ac-cessibility, namely e-mail, and seek human interaction. New Airmen in the squadron aren't going to raise a concern by walking into a com-mander's office, but they might if the commander is able to interact in their work environment. Leadership by walking around will always be a positive leadership principle.

Each of us has reacted differently to the impact technology has had on the workplace. I like to think that there are three kinds of people when dealing with technology: pessimists, optimists, and realists. The technology pessimists are those people who resist any change due to improved technologies. Technology optimists jump at the earliest op-portunity to implement any technological advancement. Technology realists, who make up the lion's share of us all, accept that change is necessary and work to integrate improvements, but they don't con-tinually search for and implement emerging technology.

Our organizations need all three technology types in order to run smoothly. It is incumbent upon each of us to understand what kind of technologist we—and those whom we work around—are. This is simply another medium where one size won't fit all. Leaders must adapt their style, depending on whom they deal with and the nature of the task to be performed. The pessimist might not "hear" the things communicated electronically. By the same token, resist the tempta-tion to always communicate electronically with the optimist. Instead, push for the personal touch and realize that your approach must be different for each person.

In essence, leadership is the challenge of inspiring the people in an organization on a goal-oriented journey. Technology enables that journey, and we, as leaders, must successfully manage both the benefits and detriments of that evolution. Ultimately, leaders are still responsible for themselves, their people, and the results of their units. It's how they can make a difference, both in the lives of their people and in the unit's mission.

It's Your Turn

In the end, a leader's true mission is to achieve a desired effect. As a result, I always approach each new assignment or responsibility with two main goals: to leave the campground better than I found it and to make a positive difference in people's lives. Working toward these goals—in concert with the Air Force's core values—helps us all to be servant leaders, focusing on others ahead of ourselves while accomplishing the mission.

Once again, let me emphasize that these principles, like the others I've written about through the years, are merely my observations. They are—in no way—*the single* best way to lead nor are any of them unique or earth-shattering. These leadership principles are merely things I've noticed from other leaders who influenced me. I encourage each of you to develop your own set of leadership principles and share them with others. Not only will it help you become a more effective leader, it will also make our Air Force even stronger than it is today.

PART 2

Articles for Senior Leaders

The following articles for senior leaders were written by General Lorenz during his tenure as the Air University commander.

Transforming Air Force Education
for the Long War and Beyond

Air University (AU) is currently in the process of transforming for the "long war" and beyond. The idea of a university reorganizing for war may seem odd, but in the Western way of war, warriors and academics have always enjoyed a close relationship. The West's first great general, Alexander, was tutored by Aristotle; when he went to war, he did so with academics in his train. According to noted military historian Victor Davis Hanson, the close relationship between warriors and scholars in the Western way of war is one of the main reasons for its success across the millennia.[1]

In the US military, the connection between thinkers and fighters has become closer than ever, and exploiting this relationship to the fullest is vital to winning the current war. Doing so, however, will require (1) understanding how military education differs from the traditional civilian model and (2) reorganizing our present system of military education to meet the emerging challenge.

The Unique Nature of Military Education

At its core, the US system of military education does not significantly differ from the civilian system. Both are based on the university model of research and teaching that has dominated Western education for centuries. In this model, professors conduct research to push their fields forward. They produce books and articles that they subsequently teach to their students and, in the process, become better educators themselves. This procedure, which systematically turns out better students, faculty, and ideas, has played a significant role in the explosion of knowledge in the West and is largely responsible for the lightning pace of innovation in science and technology today.

Military education, however, differs from most academic fields in a number of ways. First, although hundreds or thousands of schools offer instruction in most fields of study, in the United States only a handful of joint/service schools teach military art and science. Further

A version of this article was published as "Transforming Air Force Education for the Long War and Beyond," *Air and Space Power Journal* 21, no. 2 (Summer 2007): 5–9.

restricting the breadth of the field, for the most part only those schools associated with certain service sponsors have faculties knowledgeable about particular domains of war. Thus, for instance, we have only one air war college, one land war college, and one naval war college—a situation that places an enormous burden on service-school faculties to research and publish work related to the type of war for which their service is responsible. In most fields of study, if professors do not publish, they can fall back on books and articles published elsewhere to stay current and educate their students. At service schools, however, they are often the only game in town.

A second difference between military schools and the majority of civilian schools involves pure versus applied research. In most fields of study, professors write for academic audiences. Promotion, tenure, and other benefits come from moving academic debates forward. In the civilian world, outside of business, law, and engineering schools, writing for policy makers and practitioners may even have negative connotations since it might appear to sully an instructor's credentials as an unbiased observer. However, in military education this relationship is reversed, with practitioners constituting our most important audiences. Military schools conduct, or should conduct, their most highly regarded research for policy makers in Washington, generals in the field, and students in the classroom. Though important, purely academic work does not have the pride of place it enjoys at civilian schools.

A third difference involves urgency. The ideas that we in a military university explore through research and the lessons we teach often pay off—for good or ill—much faster than in other fields of study. For instance, a school's decision about whether to drop classes on conventional war and add lessons on insurgency this semester or to wait for another year can mean the difference between life and death; its results will show up on the battlefield with the next graduating class. This fact can place more pressure on our schools to change curricula and on military professors to develop new areas of knowledge and expertise than is the norm at civilian schools.

A fourth difference concerns the need to educate a larger portion of our workforce. Both civilian and military sectors desire more educated workers, but we have a stronger impetus. In modern warfare, particularly during times of rapid change, education acts as a massive power multiplier. Today the US military needs flexible and innovative thinkers almost as much as it needs bombs and bullets. Yet realistically, until fairly recently we have had enough resources to educate only a small fraction of the force. The issue of increasing the size of the educated force carries high stakes.

The Need for Change

Currently the United States finds itself in the midst of geopolitical changes that tax the flexibility of our system of military education. After 9/11, the nation's military schools worked to integrate lessons on terrorism into their curricula. As the war in Iraq heated up, they added seminars on insurgency. Yet today our schools face an underlying problem vastly greater than updating curricula and changing lessons. Essentially, we confront adaptable enemies who sometimes innovate faster than our own capacity to do so. Stateless organizational structures, ongoing cyber wars, and remote-controlled improvised explosive devices are only the most recent outputs of our enemies' idea-generating systems. Using innovations produced by these systems, they have found ways to circumvent our ponderous Cold War military apparatus and have pinned down our forces across the globe. Their flexibility at times trumps our material advantages. All too often our enemies appear to be winning this war of innovation.

To answer our opponents, we must improve our system's ability to produce and disseminate new ideas. This new system must have two parts: it must systematically generate relevant new ideas, injecting them into national debates, and it must develop adaptive, innovative students who can continue the process after they leave our military schools.

AU has begun to play a role in this war of ideas, but doing so requires significant changes. The core of our strategy at Maxwell AFB, Alabama, calls for reenergizing the university model of research and teaching that so effectively propels innovation in the civilian sector. This approach is not new to the Air Force. Throughout the 1930s, the Air Corps Tactical School employed it in an effort to confront the specter of a rising Germany and Japan and to develop new uses for emerging airpower technology. Using a combination of theory, history, and field research, instructors at the school wrote the plan employed by the United States in World War II and educated Airmen who developed strategies used by the Air Force for the next half century. Unfortunately at some point during the Cold War, AU reduced its emphasis on this spirit of innovation and outreach to national policy makers. For the most part, the Air Force outsourced service-related research on military strategy to independent think tanks, and the university became mainly a teaching school.

This neglect of innovation has proved costly to the nation as well as to our faculty and students. Although the Air Force remains the world leader in developing military technology, it lags behind the Army in its ability to produce and disseminate thoughts about how to use its new technology and ideas. By one count, for every book published on airpower today, five appear on ground-centered military solutions. In 2006 the Strategic Studies Institute—the Army War College's in-house think tank—produced 53 monographs, but during the same period, AU's tiny think tank produced only two.

When it comes to injecting ideas into national debates, we find ourselves similarly behind. For example, of the military experts regularly featured on Fox News and CNN, Soldiers outnumber Airmen five to one, and the vast majority of newspaper articles on airpower derive from interviews with ground-power experts. This lack of research production also has secondary consequences. Today the percentage of AU professors with a strong grasp of air, space, and cyberspace theory and history is small compared to the percentage of land-power experts at Army or Marine schools. At times this dearth of experience shows up in the classroom. I firmly believe that each military school has a duty to develop and disseminate new ideas about the ways its service can assist the nation and contribute to the joint fight in the long war. AU has not done as well as it could in this area.

Transforming Air University for War

To bring us back into the war of ideas, AU has begun changing the way it does business. We are treating this endeavor as part of the war effort. Success will require an integrated campaign involving numerous approaches.

First, we are reorganizing our command structure. Although the Air Force originally collocated its schools at Maxwell AFB specifically to develop synergies, at present little overlap exists among the schools. Primarily, a command structure with too large a span of control drives this lack of lateral communication. By centralizing staffs and decreasing such spans, we hope to increase synergy among the schools and enhance their accountability to our Air Force, the joint community, and the nation.

The second set of changes involves providing our instructors with greater resources and incentives to publish on topics related to air, space, and cyberspace. To do this, we are building a new university research institute—an initiative taken by the other services decades ago with good results. We believe that this institute will go a long way toward generating and disseminating ideas about ways the Air Force can contribute to national security. In line with the university model of research and teaching, the institute will have a second purpose: giving AU professors with innovative air-, space-, and cyberspace-oriented research agendas time away from the classroom to conduct their work. Doing so will not only increase our pool of researchers, but also will improve our faculty—and hence the education we offer our students.

On a similar note, we are taking significant steps to give our professors incentives to conduct research on Air Force–related topics. Ironically, in the system that has evolved (partially because of the small audience for air-related publications), instructors often have greater incentives to research topics unrelated to the Air Force than to examine questions pertaining to air, space, and cyberspace.

Similarly, publications aimed solely at academic readers often receive more credit than work intended for policy audiences. Beyond this, the knowledge and expertise that active duty students and instructors bring back fresh from the field often go unheeded because these warriors do not possess academic-level writing skills. To correct these problems, we are asking the schools to reconsider how they reward research and promote professors. Research specifically pertaining to ways that air, space, and cyberspace can contribute to the joint fight will receive the highest honors. Applied research—white papers, group endeavors, and similar projects—will receive as much credit as purely academic work. Skilled writers who coauthor with instructors and students possessing practical experience will receive as much credit as do those who prefer to work alone. These changes should help vector research toward the war effort.

Producing ideas, however, is not enough. To be effective, they must be disseminated to the nation's intellectual centers, so we have launched a number of initiatives to facilitate this process. Every year our students and faculty write hundreds of papers—most of which either appear in forums read solely by academics or disappear onto library shelves. To correct this problem, we have begun to guide student research in directions that answer current questions related to the Department of Defense (DOD), the Air Force, and the joint community and to catalogue as well as track papers produced at AU so that relevant audiences can locate them online. We have also created a requirement that students and faculty summarize their work in "blue darts"—short op-eds or influence articles—that we can forward to the DOD, joint service, or media audiences, as appropriate. Beyond this, we have begun to stand up special research teams that can rapidly respond to high-level research taskings, ensuring that DOD, joint, and Air Force policy makers can reach back to AU for information and expert opinions.

On a more academic front, we have recently launched a new journal, *Strategic Studies Quarterly*, to help promote debate on high-level policy issues and have created a new online e-mail publication, *The Wright Stuff*, to quickly disseminate research and ideas to the Air Force audience and beyond. We are also experimenting with a number of other initiatives. We have begun to commission studies on important topics from well-known authors. In addition, we are once again sponsoring symposia that bring policy makers and academics together to discuss important issues and are partnering with civilian and military universities as well as think tanks to help stimulate research and debate on Air Force–related issues. Taken together, these steps and others like them should increase the flow of ideas dealing with air, space, and cyberspace to audiences that can use them. Over time these changes will substantially increase the number and quality of relevant new ideas flowing out of AU. They will also help develop our faculty and improve the education we offer students.

The third approach aims directly at our student body. As the United States begins to understand the nature of the long war, the need for training in language and regional cultures has become even more apparent. Accordingly, over the last year, we have substantially increased our offerings in these areas. To support the Air Force's new cyber mission, the Air Force Institute of Technology will soon supplement its current graduate curriculum in cyber operations with a 12-month program in cyber warfare. Much like the Air Corps Tactical School's efforts to pioneer air war in the 1930s, this hands-on initiative engages faculty and students in a combined effort to develop technology and doctrine for fighting in cyberspace. We have also added to the number of courses in other relevant fields such as counterterrorism, counter-insurgency, space, and cyber warfare. Finally, we are currently in the process of revamping our Air and Space Basic Course to do a better job of building the confidence and a warrior ethos that will serve our junior officers for the rest of their careers.

Lastly, we are taking steps to add dramatically to the number of students we educate. Through partnerships with civilian schools, we have been able to exponentially increase the educational opportunities for enlisted Airmen. By 2008 we will begin to offer them the opportunity to pursue a bachelor's degree. Our new distance-learning program will soon allow us to give all officers a chance to pursue an AU master's degree by the 12th year of their careers. We are also attempting to create a new AU PhD in strategic studies—the first of its kind in the US military—that will greatly increase the pool of doctorate-holding officers from which the Air Force will draw its future senior leaders. Beyond this, we are making major changes in our education of junior officers and in our noncommissioned officer academies as well as taking advantage of new cyber technology to develop communities of practice for squadron commanders. Our goal in all of this is to increase vastly the number of flexible and innovative thinkers in the Air Force.

Conclusion

In sum, the United States has only now begun to come to grips with the nature of the long war and what lies beyond. Winning this war will require us to leverage our existing strengths. It will require new equipment, new tactics, and, from time to time, even new strategy. But it also requires something more. Our best hope for succeeding in this struggle lies in developing a system that institutionalizes innovation. More than anything else, we need new ideas as well as men and women who, understanding the problems we face, can innovate and adapt to overcome them. The system of military education we continue to pioneer at AU will take a significant step toward developing this system and, over the long run, defeating our opponents.

Notes

1. Victor Davis Hanson, *Carnage and Culture: Landmark Battles in the Rise of Western Power* (New York: Doubleday, 2001), chap. 5.

Accountability in Public Life

It is cruel, this accountability of good and well-intentioned men.

—"On the Collision of Wasp and Hobson"
Wall Street Journal

December 2008—"Accountability" is a loaded word in public life. It is usually associated with failures and firings (and, some might add, "scapegoating"). Given this negative connotation, if we were asked if we wanted to be "held accountable" for something, we would probably not volunteer.

Yet, that is exactly what we do when those of us who are appointed to senior offices accept the responsibility for leadership of a public institution. For us, it's imperative to understand that holding people accountable can seem cruel, yet it is essential for maintaining the public trust. Let me explain why.

I've learned that there are three levels of accountability in public life. The first level is that of the individual in public service. To be individually accountable is to be subject to the consequences of our own choices. If we choose to do the right thing, we typically receive positive consequences. In fact, it is important to understand that holding people accountable must include rewarding good behavior and performance. When we choose not to do the right thing, however, we can expect negative consequences. This is often what we associate with the word *accountability*. For most of us, making the right personal and professional choices is simply a matter of living according to the established institutional standards. These standards are usually written down and are clearly stated. There is little guesswork involved. We simply have to choose to adhere to the standards.

When we are assigned responsibility for others as a supervisor or commander, we assume a higher level of accountability—the second level. We become accountable for the choices of our people. Most of us learn rather quickly that we must set the right example for our people. We must also enforce the standards—preferably at the lowest level before minor discrepancies grow into major ones. As leaders, we also get some room to adjust the standards higher than the minimum. For example, I've always found that when my units had high standards, they had high morale, so I intentionally adjusted our expectations higher. Nevertheless, the minimum standards were clear, and we all knew what they were.

There is a third level of accountability for those who rise to be senior leaders in a public organization like the US Air Force. This level is fundamentally different. We are still accountable for our own choices and those of our people, but we are also accountable for outcomes.

In our business, results matter; senior leaders are accountable for results. We can have the right intentions and work hard, but results speak for themselves. Furthermore, when things go terribly wrong, senior leaders are accountable, whether or not they had any direct personal involvement. If this seems cold and cruel, that's because sometimes it is.

Perhaps the best explanation of this level of accountability is a 1952 *Wall Street Journal* editorial written after the USS *Hobson* and the USS *Wasp* collided. The commanding officer of the *Hobson* had gone to sleep, leaving his subordinates to run the bridge. He was awoken as the two ships approached each other; in his disorientation, he gave a steering command that, in retrospect, was fatal. His last command took the ship right in front of the *Wasp*. When the ships ran together, the *Hobson* was cut in two and sank within four minutes. The captain, and 176 of her crew, drowned as a result. The Navy convened a board of inquiry to assign accountability for the incident. Many believed that it was unfair to assign blame to an exemplary officer whose intentions could not have included such terrible consequences.

In response, the *Wall Street Journal* editorial staff wrote, "This accountability is not for intention, but for the deed. The captain of a ship, like the captain of a state, is given honor and privileges and trust beyond other men. But let him steer the wrong course, let him touch ground, let him bring disaster to his ship or to his men, and he must answer for what he has done. No matter what, he cannot escape. It is cruel, this accountability of good and well-intentioned men."[1]

Like the captain of a ship or the pilot of an aircraft, senior leaders are responsible for setting the right course for their institutions in a dangerous, uncertain world. Unlike lower-level supervisors and junior commanders, they often have little written guidance on how to do this.

These leaders are responsible for charting the course for their institutions, and they are accountable for the results, although they cannot possibly predict the future with certainty. For many years to come, people will second-guess their decisions with the benefit of hindsight. Suffering this second-guessing is part of being a senior leader, and it is something all strategic leaders must come to grips with.

We have chosen to assign this level of accountability to our senior leaders. It is a tough choice, but, as the *Wall Street Journal* article explains, "The choice is that or an end to responsibility and, finally . . . an end to the confidence and trust in the men who lead, for men will not long trust leaders who feel themselves beyond accountability for what they do."[2]

This is the reason for assigning such a high level of accountability for senior leaders of public institutions. Accountability is essential for trust. We risk losing the trust of the American people if we do not hold ourselves accountable. When things go wrong, the American people need to see that we take action to correct the problems. But we must also evaluate the situation and, as appropriate, assign accountability for those responsible. Sometimes, accountability should be assigned to senior leaders. This is especially true when we find problems that are "systemic" in nature. Only our senior leaders have the ability to find and fix systemic problems, even if they were not personally involved in the incidents that brought these problems to light. Our leaders are responsible and accountable for charting the right course for the institution. When the institution strays, senior leaders must be held accountable.

This can be cruel, but we are dealing with a Hobson's choice, which is really no choice at all. We either accept this level of accountability or risk losing trust. Accountability, especially for our senior leaders, is the price we pay to establish and maintain trust.

Given current events, the time may have come for private institutions to learn this important lesson. Indeed, it is becoming increasingly apparent that decisions made by business institutions such as those in the financial sector affect the public welfare for good or ill. This development is reinforced by the investment that Americans, acting through their elected representatives, are willing to make in private corporations. As these "private" institutions are increasingly expected to act in the public interest, they will have to build public trust. If they want to do this in a lasting way, they will have to grapple with the subject of accountability. Perhaps they should look to the wisdom of an old *Wall Street Journal* editorial as they do so.

Notes

1. "On the Collision of Wasp and Hobson," *Wall Street Journal*, 14 May 1952.
2. Ibid.

Leadership Principles for Senior Leaders

August 2009—In 1987 I was commander of the 93rd Air Refueling Squadron at Castle AFB, California. Late one night, I sat down and wrote out a list of leadership principles. There was nothing magical about them—they were simply useful precepts I had learned over the years. I added to those principles in the summer of 2005 as the director of financial management and comptroller at the Pentagon and again, in the spring of 2008, as the commander of AU. As the commander of AETC, I published monthly articles, short vignettes, detailing the application of the leadership principles that have guided me through the years.

I have never sought to instill my leadership principles on others. Rather, I've tried to motivate others to reflect on the leadership principles that have guided them, to write them down, and to develop them. I've tried to help them use their principles to develop those within their command and to push their organizations towards greater success.

That said, I offer the following for consideration.

Never Develop a Sense of Entitlement

As senior leaders in the Air Force, you are entitled to certain privileges. Those privileges exceed what most Air Force personnel are authorized. Although the privileges come with increased responsibility, others won't always see it that way. A large dose of humility can go a long way. After all, an organization's success depends on all of its members keeping their egos in check.

A leader must be able to connect with subordinates and communicate from a shared common vision that everyone can comprehend and accept. It is always easier to communicate your vision by talking about an experience or using an analogy that everyone can relate to, understand, and remember. It is critical that leaders deliver their message in easily grasped terminology.

If you ever get the feeling that "you deserve" something or that the organization "owes you," immediately stop what you're doing, take a

---

A version of this article was delivered to the Senior Leader Orientation Course.

deep breath, and reevaluate the situation. The "me" path is a dangerous one, and once you start heading in that direction, it can be hard to turn around. Over the course of my career in the Air Force, I've seen a number of people develop an entitlement attitude, only to end up disappointed and bitter. When this happens, the person loses; his or her family loses; and, ultimately, the organization loses.

Creating Candor

It is essential that candor be a part of every organization. Candor helps us to identify our blind spots. Everyone has them—areas where we think things are better than they are, areas where we're a little too confident. To find the blind spots, we must encourage dissenting opinions and negative feedback. We should ask our organizations open-ended questions: "What are we missing?" "How can we do this better?" "What's the downside?" "What will other people say?" When our people answer, we must welcome their inputs, even when those inputs don't cast our leadership in the best light.

As followers, we must work at creating candor as well. While the leader must set the tone for open communication, it is important that those who voice dissenting opinions or give negative feedback do so in a way that it can have the most effect. When voicing your disagreement, propose a solution or alternative path. If you are pointing out a blind spot for one of your leaders, strongly consider doing it in private. This is especially true if the issue is more personal in nature. It's much easier for a leader to listen to a criticism made in private.

In the end, our time as leaders will be judged by the quality of our decisions and the accomplishments of our people. The personal price we pay in the short term for creating candor in our organizations is well worth the long-term professional and institutional benefits of hearing the best ideas and illuminating our blind spots.

Accountability

If we were asked if we wanted to be "held accountable" for something, we would probably not want to volunteer. Yet that is exactly what we do when those of us appointed to senior offices accept the responsibility for leadership of a public institution. For us, it is imperative to understand that holding people accountable can seem cruel but is an essential ingredient toward maintaining the public trust.

When we are assigned responsibility for others as a commander, we assume a higher level of accountability. We become accountable for the choices of our people. Most of us learn rather quickly that we must set the right example for our people. We must also enforce the standards, at all levels, before minor discrepancies grow into major ones. I've always found that units with high standards also have high morale.

In addition to being responsible for the choices of others, senior leaders are accountable for the outcomes and results of those choices whether or not they had any direct personal involvement. In our business, results matter, and even the best intentions cannot erase poor results. If this seems cold and cruel, that's because sometimes it is.

Accountability is essential for trust. We risk losing the trust of the American public if we do not hold ourselves and our people accountable. When things go wrong, the public needs to see that we took action to correct the problem. Many times, accountability is assigned directly to senior leaders. This is especially true when we find problems that are "systemic" in nature. Only our senior leaders have the ability to find and fix systemic problems, even if they were not personally involved in the incidents that brought these problems to light. We either accept this level of accountability or risk losing trust. Accountability, especially for our senior leaders, is the price we pay to establish and maintain the public trust.

Objective Decision Making

Making decisions is something leaders do each and every day. Most decisions are made without much thought, almost unconsciously and, in many cases, automatically. Others, however, are decisions that involve time and thought and can impact more than just ourselves. These are the decisions where the process is an art, and it defines who we are as leaders.

First, and foremost, effective decisions require objectivity. The old adage, "the more objective you are, the more effective you are," has never been more accurate or applicable than it is today. It can be tempting to look at decisions through the lens of a small straw. Effective leaders must step back and gain a much broader view; they must open their aperture. I've always advocated looking at issues and decisions from the viewpoint of your boss's boss. This approach helps to open the aperture and maintain objectivity. After all, if your boss's boss is happy with your boss, then your boss will be happy with you.

In order to gain the broad objective view, leaders must work to gather a complete picture of the situation. That awareness involves considering all the variables weighing into the decision, competing interests involved in the decision, and determining the potential consequences. The potential consequences must include possible second- and third-order consequences. Tough calls like these can involve individuals, organizations, and issues beyond those initially thought. Weigh the consequences against unit missions and organizational goals. Investigate how the decision will move things forward in the near, mid, and long term. This will provide the context for the decision and, although it will involve a lot of work, will result in the broadest view of the entire process.

Lastly, tough decisions can be very emotional. Don't let emotion play into the decision-making process. Emotion only serves to cloud the issue and, potentially, can result in a decision where near-term happiness fades quickly into mid- and long-term unintended challenges. Leaders must look at decisions from the outside, unattached to the emotional influence from within. Leaders must rise above such distractions in order to maintain their objectivity.

Leaders use decision making to define reality. Decisions made within context and with the benefit of situational awareness will position future issues for success and establish tomorrow's realities for our subordinates, our boss, and, ultimately, our boss's boss. In the end, objectivity will ensure that decisions will result in the desired effect and will keep you and your organization headed in the "best" direction.

Lean Times

You don't need to pick up a newspaper to know that our nation and our Air Force face challenging economic times in the months and years ahead. Leading in lean times requires making tough choices, but this is what leaders do. If you've ever heard me discuss leadership, then you have heard me say that leaders must learn the art of balancing shortfalls. We never have enough time, money, or manpower. This is true in our personal lives as well as our professional positions.

We often use tools to help us. One tool I have found to be indispensible is the "unfunded requirements list." This list includes all of the projects and upgrades for your organization that are not in the budget. This list must be comprehensive and part of a multiyear plan for improvement. Most importantly, it must be a priority order. In order to accurately prioritize the requirements, tie each of them to either core, sustainable, or enhanced tasks. The core tasks are things you have to do to accomplish your mission and are the most essential. Your goal is to work down the items on the list one at a time—focus on the top priority until you get the resources required and then go to the next item. You should be ready to execute the top priority at any moment; you never know when the resources will be available.

In lean times, we must protect the core tasks. This means being ruthless in cutting the enhanced items first, and then figuring out workarounds when sustainable items have to go. Sometimes we may have to implement a workaround that is uncomfortable, but we must in order to protect the mission and core tasks.

Develop Your Vision

Our job, as leaders, is to make people's dreams come true each and every day. I know you all have dreams, visions that could benefit our Airmen both today and tomorrow. Such visions must be pursued—you should never, ever, ever give up.

In order to realize a vision, several things need to happen. First, you must align the vision with one of the core functions I mentioned earlier. The closer to the core, the easier it will be to gain support and, eventually, resourcing. Next, take the vision and develop a strategy. Depending on your vision, the strategy may involve acquisition, implementation, execution, modification, or one of many other aspects. Let your strategy start at the 40 percent solution, evolve to 80 percent, and remain at 98 percent. Realize that the process is continual—you will never get to 100 percent.

With the strategy in place, you can start socializing the vision. Socialization will also help your vision progress and grow roots through increased organizational support and understanding. The support will help you champion the concept for resourcing. After all, your vision must have resourcing in order to come true. Those resources will go to winners, not to losers—invest the time and energy to be a winner.

In life, and especially in the Air Force, priorities and personnel are always changing. Over time, your vision will need to adapt to the realities of change. It will require even greater persistence and objectivity. Giving your vision roots and aligning it with core functions will create something that can be handed off and sustained through change. The best ideas, sustained by hard work, can be carried forward by any leader.

You may also find yourself joining an organization and accepting other people's visions. In this situation, evaluate their vision against current realities and resourcing priorities. If they've done their homework, the project will be easy to move forward. If they haven't, assess the vision to determine if it should move ahead or if its time has passed.

Our Air Force needs you to champion your visions, to develop them along our service core functions, and to socialize them—let them grow roots and evolve. Do your homework and the resources will follow. After all, it is your initiatives that fuel the positive change that makes our Air Force the finest in the world.

What Will Your Leadership Legacy Be?

As I said before, the most important point about these leadership principles that I have laid out is to encourage others to define their own principles. I hope to motivate and aid our service's leaders in identifying and clarifying their positions, not in memorizing mine. In order for a leader's set of principles to be effective, they should be based on a foundation—such as the ideals embodied in the Air Force's core values—and they must reflect who that leader is. As senior leaders in today's Air Force, continue to develop and articulate your principles; you will never regret it, and it will make you better leaders for our nation.

PART 3

Articles from US Air Force Academy Association of Graduates *Checkpoints* Magazine

Never, Ever Give Up:
A Story of Educational Perseverance

Winter 2009—In order to succeed at the US Air Force Academy, cadets must excel at academic, athletic, and military challenges. One of the toughest lessons all cadets learn during the four years is how to balance their natural strengths—the things they enjoy being good at—with everything else. In essence, this balancing act paves the way for success in service to the nation after graduation. Resting only on our strengths makes us one-dimensional leaders. Our country needs leaders who are able to engage in many dimensions. For me, I learned very quickly that I was going to have to work hardest in the "academic dimension." It ended up being one of my greatest struggles.

The journey actually began in the summer of 1960 when I was only nine years old. My father was a captain in the Air Force, stationed at Lowry AFB in Denver, Colorado. One Saturday, he drove my entire family down to Colorado Springs, and we visited the Air Force Academy for the very first time. I remember it like it was yesterday because that was the day I fell in love with the Academy. Construction on Cadet Chapel had yet to begin, and Sijan Hall was still years in the future. I remember standing there, under the bright blue mountain sky, and pledging to myself that one day this was the place I would go to school. As a fourth grader, I did not know how I was going to get there, but I knew right then and there that I was going to devote all my energy to becoming a cadet at the most beautiful school I had ever seen.

During the next nine years, through eight moves and eight different schools (including four high schools), I followed my father across the country and around the world. During that entire time, I kept my goal in sight to become a cadet at the Air Force Academy. I joined every high school club. I tried out for every sport I could participate in. I took every course the Academy required. I even ran for every high school office that was available. This was particularly tough because we were moving almost every year. I took the ACT and then the

A version of this article was published as "Never, Ever Give Up," *Checkpoints*, December 2009, 21–22.

SAT—five times! If there was anything that I thought would improve my chances to get into the Academy, I did it!

When it finally came time to get an appointment to the Academy, I immediately applied to Illinois, my home state. My congressman wrote back that even with all my hard work, I was fourth in line for an appointment and that I should try again next year. I was disappointed and somewhat discouraged but vowed not to give up. I talked to the Academy group, which was then in Washington, DC, and they told me that some congressional districts did not have qualified candidates. They recommended that I should also apply to those districts. My dad was stationed in Washington at the time, so I literally started walking the halls of Congress until I came upon the office of Cong. Tim Lee Carter of Kentucky's 5th Congressional District. He had no qualified candidate that year and, after I had a face-to-face meeting with the congressman, nominated me to the Academy to be a member of the class of 1973. I was on top of the world! On 23 June 1969, on a bright, shiny day, I reported to the base of the ramp with 1,403 of my new classmates.

Basic Cadet Training was a blur. We ran everywhere, from dawn until dusk. Upper classmen yelled at us all day long. It seemed we were in constant motion 24 hours a day. However, I was happy. I had achieved my life's goal and was a cadet at the US Air Force Academy. It had been a challenge to get into the Academy, but I was now a cadet, and I thought the hardest part was over. Boy was I wrong! Little did I know that the hard part was just beginning.

It started when we took the battery of aptitude tests that seemed to go on forever. I did well in the social sciences and ended up validating the entire fourth class year of history, and my political science scores were well up there. However, in the math and science areas of the core curriculum, I was at the bottom of the heap. My math scores entitled me to be placed in all the "peoples" courses. Anything that had a "101" attached to it and was a "bucket" section was where they sent me. I slugged my way through one math and science course after another. I had more extra instruction sessions in physics than actual classroom sessions and still ended up with a "D." I think they did not give me an "F" because they felt sorry for me.

I survived my fourth class year, but the "bucket" sections were getting smaller as many of our classmates resigned or were "academically" asked to leave. Third class academic year began, and for the first time, I really understood what challenging academics were. The

11 semester hours of the "peoples" Math 201 were pure drudgery. I just barely survived that onslaught, when Computer Science 200 snuck up on me, and I met my first academic board with a big fat "F." It was quite a humbling experience to stand at attention in front of 13 captains, majors, and colonels justifying why I should stay at the academy. Since I had validated fourth class history and it appeared that my military order of merit was adequate, they voted to keep me for one more semester to see how I would do. I passed Computer Science 200 on my second try and slid into second class summer. It had gotten to the point that I was living semester to semester and looking forward to summer training because I knew I could make it through the military training without too much trouble.

Second class academics began, and I was finally getting into some history and political science courses that were actually enjoyable. In fact, political science classes were so enjoyable that I declared international affairs as my major. However, two gigantic math and science hurdles remained. A solid year of electrical engineering (EE) and aeronautical engineering stood like the Rocky Mountains between me and graduation. Two other things that were about to affect my future time as a cadet were also out there, but being 19 years old, I did not see them coming. The first was that I was now truly at the bottom of my class in the math and science areas. All the other cadets who had, for two years, cushioned my grades at the bottom of the bell curve were gone. The second was that I had finally met a young lady. Yes, now when I needed to be truly focused on studying to make it to the end, I started dating. During the middle of the week when I should have been studying, I was now talking on the telephone. Every weekend, I was faced with the choice of studying for courses I truly disliked or going downtown to date this young lady. Being 19, I found that the choice was, of course, obvious! As the fall semester started slipping by and I prepared for finals and Christmas leave, I had a very uneasy feeling.

On 23 December 1971, I arrived at McConnell AFB, Kansas, on Christmas leave to visit my parents. I told my dad that I was "concerned" about my grades. This turned out to be an understatement. Early on Christmas Eve, he called my academic advisor and asked him to find out what my grades were. My advisor checked and called my dad back immediately. He said I had done well in history and political science and had earned a 2.0 grade point average for the semester, but I had flunked both EE and aeronautical engineering! He also said that the academic board would be meeting to decide my fate the day after Christmas. He told my dad that things did not look good.

Needless to say, this was not a very happy Christmas for me and my parents. I spent all day praying that I would be allowed to stay at the Academy to redeem myself and to earn those golden lieutenant bars. The hours passed by so very slowly. On the afternoon of the 26th, my advisor called my dad and said that because of my Military Order of Merit, the academic board had voted to let me stay. However, I would be restricted to the cadet area for six months and would have to take R-Flight (summer school) my first class summer to graduate with my class. The Academy board had given me another chance. I was so thankful, but I was about to learn some very valuable lessons during the next six months.

When I got back to the "zoo," I found out that 17 of my classmates had flunked out that semester; I was still at the Academy by the grace of God and the dean. I also found out that I was assigned six (the maximum number) weekend academic call to quarters (WACQ). Each WACQ was two and a half hours long, which meant in addition to all the military duties that occurred each weekend, I also had to be at my desk studying a minimum of 18 hours from Friday night until the Sunday evening call to quarters. This was easier said than done, especially during the dark ages. I remember sitting at my desk studying EE (for the second time) and watching my classmates leave the squadron area to go on dates downtown. After about a month of this, my initial euphoria of getting to stay at the academy passed, and I started to get depressed. I began to ask myself, "Is all this pain worth it?" I hated EE and aeronautical engineering; I was never going to use these "worthless" classes. I told myself that the core curriculum was a waste of time. I was on the verge of resigning, but a group of people and a piece of precious metal changed my mind.

That group of people included my family, air officer commanding (AOC), professors, and classmates who helped and encouraged me during this challenging time. They assisted me in studying for my classes and motivated me when I was down. They all made a real difference in focusing and improving my spirits. However, I will never forget the day my squadron ordered class rings. I remember trying on that piece of precious metal for the first time. It was so big, heavy, and beautiful. They gave me an order form with a picture of the '73 class crest. I thought it was magnificent. I took the order form and taped it to the wall in front of my desk. From then on, when I started to feel sorry for myself, I would look at the picture of that beautiful ring and remind myself why I came to the Academy in the first place. I started to count down the days until the ring dance: 100 days, 98, 50, 25, and so on. Finally the great day arrived. That night when I put the ring on for the first time, I knew all the hard work had been worth it and that the Academy had shaped my life forever.

The semester that I had been "locked" in my room for six months, I achieved my highest grades. That summer "R-Flight" went well, even though I did not get any leave. My firstie (senior) year was still challenging, but there was nothing that could get in the way of those gold bars. On 6 June 1973, 564 of my classmates preceded me in getting their diplomas handed to them by Sen. Barry Goldwater of Arizona, with a total of 844 of us getting to walk across the stage. After four long, hard years, I had finally made it, earning an Academy degree and the coveted golden lieutenant bars.

I have had a lot of time over the 36 years since graduation to reflect on how the entire Academy experience affected me and shaped my life. Like everyone else, I have faced personal and professional challenges. But even on the darkest of days, I looked back and remembered the WACQs, EE, and aeronautical engineering. If I could make it through the Academy's academic challenges, then I could make it through anything.

Like most graduates, I internalized the honor code as a daily "code of conduct." However, I left the Academy with other major life lessons as well. The first was that you must "never, ever, ever give up." If you are willing to work hard and stay focused, tenacity and perseverance will help you prevail. The second was that the pursuit of learning through education, even during the dreaded core curriculum, is a major building block for success in life. You see, taking courses is not about the grades; it is about what you learn and how you use that learning in your everyday life. We all must never stop learning and growing. To this day, I am always reading and studying. Finally, achieving any great endeavor is all about teamwork. If it were not for my parents, family, professors, advisors, and classmates that helped me graduate from the academy, I would not have been able to serve our nation in the world's greatest air force.

As I said at the beginning of this article, one of the toughest lessons to learn at the Academy is to balance one's natural strengths across the academic, athletic, and military dimensions. I used to think my challenges were unique, but as the years have passed, I have observed that many, if not most, cadets had similar challenges in one or more of these three dimensions. Our graduates and the nation are all the better for it.

We Win as a Wing, We Lose as a Wing:
A Story of Spirit as a Force Multiplier

On the fields of friendly strife are sown the seeds that on other days and other fields will bear the fruits of victory.

—Gen Douglas MacArthur

Summer 2010—I will never forget the night of 9 November 1996. A well-coached Air Force Academy football team with a phenomenal quarterback solemnly walked off the field at West Point's Michie Stadium. An average Army football team had just soundly defeated them 23–7. As I looked across the field, I saw the reason why. A sea of 4,000 screaming West Point cadets decked out in Army black and gold jerseys danced in the stands, cheering as one. You see, the Army football team wasn't made up only of those wearing helmets and shoulder pads—it also included a highly organized group of cadets, cheerleaders, and its band. Together the Army team had one goal in mind: defeat Air Force!

As I followed the Air Force football team off the field, I realized that our Cadet Wing should work to have the same effect as the Army Corps of Cadets. Although the wing could not help on the field, it could have an impact from the stands. Organized and energized as the Army cadets were that night, our Cadet Wing could be worth at least three to seven points by the end of the game. In many games, those three to seven points are the difference between winning and losing.

The Air Force football team completed the 1996 season two weeks later with a final record of six wins and five losses. Of all the games that season, six of them were decided by fewer than seven points. Although we beat Notre Dame, losses to both Army and Navy forced the Academy to relinquish possession of the commander-in-chief's trophy for the first time in seven years. As the commandant of cadets, I knew we could do more to support the football team. I thought that the team would be a good unifying element within the wing and a method to increase overall morale and pride. In addition, such emphasis could benefit other intercollegiate programs as well.

A version of this article was published as "We Win as a Wing, We Lose as a Wing," *Checkpoints*, June 2010, 20–22.

We formed the Cadet Wing Esprit-de-Corps Committee co-chaired by a member of the Air Force Academy's Falcon football team and a nonintercollegiate cadet. The committee started by surveying all 40 cadet squadrons and each of the four classes to better understand the environment at the Academy. At the time, intercollegiate athletes from 27 teams comprised 25 percent of the Cadet Wing. It was an important study, and the results ended up telling a very interesting story.

The committee found that there was a significant amount of resentment between the intercollegiate and nonintercollegiate cadets. Nonintercollegiate cadets perceived that the intercollegiate athletes hid behind their privileges, like separate dining, reduced room inspections, and less time at mandatory military training events. The intercollegiate athletes expressed frustration that the nonintercollegiate cadets did not appreciate the significant time required on the practice fields. These perceived friction points between the groups would be a major hurdle in building overall wing spirit. If we wanted to make a difference on the "fields of friendly strife," we needed to move the perceptions within the wing closer together.

After assessing the study results, the Cadet Esprit de Corps Committee built a plan named "Operation Restore Thunder." Its mission was to bridge the gap between intercollegiate and nonintercollegiate cadets. The plan aimed to foster an environment within the Cadet Wing where cadets both feel and demonstrate pride in their Academy and all cadet programs.

The committee's recommendations looked at established spirit programs at Army, Navy, Texas A&M, and the Citadel and started at the top of the cadet leadership chain. They established a new cadet leadership position (wing spirit officer) and recommended that the new person work and live on wing staff with the captain of the football team. Together, these two cadet leaders were tasked to build an overall strategic campaign plan on how the entire Cadet Wing team would support not just the football team but all intercollegiate teams for the entire year. In turn, each cadet squadron adopted an intercollegiate team, and both the cadet squadron commander and the respective team captain had to brief the commandant on their yearlong strategic support plans. These plans had to be updated monthly with the commandant.

The committee also found that most cadets liked living with others that have similar tastes, backgrounds, and experiences. If we were going to get each group to understand the other's challenges and build a true wing team, we needed to get them away from this tendency and "walk in each other's shoes." What better way to do that than to live and work together? So the committee recommended a policy that aimed to "integrate" all cadets, forcing intercollegiate athletes to start living with nonintercollegiate cadets. It was not a popular policy, but over time the new roommates gained an understanding for each other's challenges.

The Cadet Wing began publishing a master calendar that included specific "games of the week." They encouraged all Academy mission elements to avoid scheduling events that conflicted with those games so that more cadets could attend and lend their support. We created cadet spirit awards and designed a blue "spirit jersey" to be worn at games. We even started preparing the battlefield during the cadet's first summer in Basic Cadet Training. The wing spirit officer gave all new cadets a briefing about specific "spirit responsibilities," telling the new cadets that they were the engine that produced the energy to keep the Academy's spirit machine running smoothly.

We instituted the Outstanding Military Athlete Award. We reinstituted car rallies and spirit dinners. After specific games, we had the coaches and team captains thank the Cadet Wing for their support. We established a weekly air tasking order (ATO) to support the teams. The ATO described the spirit plan of attack for specific games and periods of time. At every game the chief of wing spirit was responsible for coordinating the Cadet Wing, cheerleaders, and the Drum and Bugle Corps. We developed scripts for contingences at the games. The scripts further developed the ATO and described when to cheer, what to chant, and how the plan would change based on the score and phase of the game. Once again, we required that the Cadet Wing stand up in the bleachers whenever the team was on the field. When we sang the third verse of the Air Force song, the Cadet Wing went out on the football field to show solidarity with the team. The cadets formed a line and held hands with the team as the entire wing sang together.

We had plans whether we won or lost; we were always there to support the team. None of these ideas were original, but three things were different: (1) every idea fit into the cadet-built strategic spirit plan; (2) the cadets implemented all aspects of the plan; and (3) the plan had the support of the superintendent, dean, commandant, director of athletics, and the coaches. The plan supported our initial goals: improve cadet morale, build pride in the Academy, and unite all of the Academy mission elements towards a common goal—defeat the opposition! Slowly but surely the "me" mentality transformed into a "we" mentality. After all, we go to war as a team and not as individuals.

We kicked off the next football season in August 1997 with our great football coach Fisher DeBerry briefing each of the four cadet groups. Coach DeBerry emphasized how important the entire Cadet Wing was to victory. He talked about teamwork and how the Cadet Wing's energy and spirit made a difference on the field. The first game of the season was against Idaho during parents' weekend. The cadet strategic plan, the ATO, contained a day-by-day schedule that called for a car rally, a spirit dinner, and a major pep rally to build spirit in preparation for the game. It also set up a time for the wing spirit officer to utilize our new public address system to practice new cheers with the Cadet Wing, cheerleaders, and the Drum and Bugle Corps. The battle slogan became "feel the thunder," and everyone at the Academy greeted each other with that cry.

In the beginning, the fourth class cadets and those cadet leaders responsible for the plan accounted for most of the participation. Many cadets thought "spirit" was spontaneous and resisted organized motivation. The first game against Idaho was very close, but Air Force was victorious, 14–10. As we all stood on the field in Falcon Stadium, holding hands and singing the "third verse," many in the stands felt the Cadet Wing team had made a difference. The next week when we were getting ready for an away game at Rice in Houston, Texas, Coach DeBerry and the team captains thanked the Cadet Wing for the energy that helped in the victory. The wing stood and cheered. We crushed Rice 41–12. The next week, the team came back home to the Academy and squeaked by the University of Nevada–Las Vegas by just one point, 25–24. Coach DeBerry once again thanked the wing for making a difference.

Our next game was critical—against our in-state conference rival Colorado State University. The previous year, we watched a large halftime lead turn into a difficult loss at home by only one point; it was a real heartbreaker. The cadet leadership decided to pull out all the stops. The plan called for a 1,000 cadet–strong contingent to fill the stadium in Fort Collins. We ended up sending even more to the game; the setting was electric. We totally dominated the field and beat them 24–0!

We won four of the next six games. Of those games, five of them saw the game end with a margin of fewer than seven points. The next big game was now against the Army Knights at Falcon Stadium. The commander-in-chief's trophy was in play because we had previously defeated Navy by three. The ATO built up the spirit and anticipation during the week leading up to Saturday's game. There were lots of terrific spirit banners and pep rallies. We even scheduled fly-bys from both the Air Force and the Army. However, this year it was all strategically thought out and run by the cadets with one goal in mind for the Cadet Wing team—Beat Army!

The Cadet Wing marched onto the field wearing battle dress uniforms (BDU) before the game. Many in the stands thought they should have worn service dress, but it was all for effect. Right before kickoff, the entire wing removed their BDU tops, revealing bright blue Air Force spirit jerseys. The giant sea of blue stunned everyone. This was followed by 16 F-16's in afterburner that flew over during kickoff. Army never had a chance. We destroyed them 24–0. I remember walking by the West Point superintendent and commandant and exclaiming, "We stole all of your spirit ideas!" The wing continued its spirited support and helped the football team to 10 wins and a postseason bowl appearance that season. All told, the Cadet Wing was flying high.

Away from the football field, the other intercollegiate teams enjoyed the support of the 40 cadet squadrons as well. Can you imagine 75 cadets cheering on the rifle team in the middle of the week or 50 cadets showing up to support the fencing team? It happened because the cadet leadership made it happen. Now, I am not saying all the cadets bought into the strategic spirit plan, but the more they saw the positive results their efforts created, the more they wanted to participate.

The following year witnessed even more success. The football team won 12 games, finished the season nationally ranked, and crushed the Washington Huskies 45–25 in a postseason bowl game. After the last game of the regular season, the Cadet Wing approached the director of athletics and asked to tear down the goal posts in Falcon Stadium. Now, goal posts are expensive, and new ones were certainly not in the budget. I was impressed with the request and excited when the athletic director actually let them do it in the name of the Academy spirit.

More than a dozen years have passed since those young cadets built and implemented the "Operation Restore Thunder" spirit plan for the Cadet Wing. These cadets are now captains and majors in our US Air Force, and many have seen combat in Iraq and Afghanistan. They helped improve the tradition of team excellence at our Air Force Academy and have carried that winning attitude with them into their military and civilian careers. The spirit committee ended its initial briefing to the Cadet Wing with a quote from John Wooden, the well-known collegiate men's basketball coach: "Success is a peace of mind which is a direct result of self-satisfaction in knowing you did your best to become the best you are capable of becoming." I believe that all the cadets, both on and off the athletic fields, internalized this ideal. Today, our Air Force and our nation are all the better for it.

PART 4

Monthly Releases

The following commentaries were written by General Lorenz during his tenure as the Air Education and Training Command commander and following his retirement. These commentaries are part of the "Lorenz on Leadership" series.

Back to Basics

15 July 2008—These are challenging times. If you're keeping up with the news, you're probably as frustrated as I am when you see editorials with titles such as "Clean up the Air Force." While we have important issues such as nuclear accountability that must be addressed, you and I both know that the vast majority of the Air Force does not need "cleaning up." As Secretary of Defense Robert Gates has said, "I have every confidence in you, and in the Air Force that has served our country so well."[1]

Nevertheless, when faced with these negative perceptions, our best answer is to get back to basics. Every good team faces bad news from time to time. The excellent teams get through adversity by focusing on what made them excellent to begin with. This is what we must do now.

For the US Air Force, our basics have been and must always be our core values: integrity, service, and excellence. These values have stood the test of time. They sustained our predecessors when they faced difficulty, and they will do the same for us today.

Integrity is our number one value, which is why we say "integrity first." When used to describe a building, the word integrity implies strength. If a building has integrity, it can weather a storm and remain strong. The Air Force is built upon the integrity of its people—you and me. If our collective integrity is strong, then the Air Force will be able to weather any storm. Unfortunately, the opposite is true as well.

I believe the key to integrity is transparency. Our actions should be transparent to outsiders. While they may not always agree with our decisions, they will see that we are making an honest effort to do what is right. Everything we do in serving the nation should be done as if we were being observed by the American people. If we act in this way, integrity will not be a problem.

We are all public servants, and this requires sacrifice. In short, it requires us to put "service before self." We exhibit this core value when we leave our families for deployments, when we put ourselves in harm's way, and even when we work the extra hour to make sure the job is done right.

Service before self does not mean service in spite of self, however. We all have times when our personal lives, especially our families, take priority. That is when we as the Air Force family must step up and cover for each other. When you take on an additional task to help a fellow Airman who is dealing with personal issues, you make the Air Force stronger. And one day, someone will do the same for you.

We became the world's leading Air Force by exhibiting "excellence in all we do," and we must keep striving for excellence today. This means that we must aggressively and constantly seek improvement. The Airmen who came before us would not settle for the status quo. They always sought better ways of doing business—better processes, better equipment, and better training. We must do the same.

It is a fact that the most dangerous time for each of us is when we first get comfortable at something, be it flying a sortie, repairing an engine, teaching a class, or driving to work. Comfort leads to complacency, and complacency kills. For this reason, I believe that we all should be a little uncomfortable in our jobs. That slight degree of discomfort gives us a valuable edge that spurs us to learn more and get better.

Can I share a secret with you? I'm a little uncomfortable in my new position as commander of AETC. As I learn about what the great Airmen of the command do, I am truly humbled. Our command is so large and diverse that I have a hard time seeing how I can ever become as knowledgeable as I want to be.

Although I would like to be comfortable, I know that personal comfort would be professionally detrimental for the Airmen I command. That is why I'm going to leave my comfort zone, focus on the basics, and strive for bigger and better things for our team. I am just one Airman; however, I can't do anything alone.

No one says it better than our acting secretary of the Air Force, Michael Donley: "There is no quicker route to recovery than the power of tens of thousands of Airmen and civilians rededicating themselves to the high standards of excellence that have always been the hallmark of the world's best Air Force."[2] I ask you to come alongside me, and let's work together to turn adversity into opportunity by getting back to basics.

Notes

1. "Gates: Focus on Nuclear Mission," Air Force Print News, 10 June 2008.
2. Ed White, "Acting SECAF Donley Shares Perspective with Airmen," *Space Observer*, 10 July 2008.

Staying Safe in the Real World

11 August 2008—It's no secret. We're flying some old airplanes. In fact, aging airplanes continue to consume much of our attention. We are currently replacing the wing boxes on our C-130s, first delivered in 1956. Late last year, we grounded our F-15Cs, first delivered in 1974, after one literally broke apart in the sky. And more recently, we have focused on the T-38, which was first delivered in 1961.

In April, two AETC pilots died in a T-38 crash at Columbus AFB, Mississippi. The investigation board performed a thorough analysis of the wreckage, and we now know that the cause was a broken part, a lever in the wing. The lever broke as the airplane taxied, and this caused the flight controls to be ineffective on takeoff. This is the first time this part is known to have failed.

As soon as he found out about the levers, my predecessor, Gen Bill Looney, directed a halt in flying to allow inspection of every lever in the fleet. If a lever was cracked, or even if it had a nick, gouge, or scratch, our team replaced it.

But we didn't stop there. We learned that the lever suffers high stress when flight controls are moved on the ground with no power, so we stopped this practice. In addition, our T-38 pilots paused to study the accident and the malfunction. We have also teamed up with Air Force Materiel Command (AFMC) to take two important steps. First, we studied the levers in-depth to react to the original problem. More importantly, we were proactive by disassembling multiple aircraft to look for additional parts that may develop similar problems.

Because there is a very small chance that these levers may fail at some unspecified time in the future, AFMC is manufacturing new, stronger levers for all T-38s. As soon as these levers are available, we will install them.

Some people will ask, "Why don't we stop flying until these levers are ready?" It's a good question, and we did consider this. After a full discussion with commanders, flight engineers, maintenance experts, and instructor pilots, we decided that continuing to fly was the right thing to do. In making this decision, we weighed the risk of flying with that of not flying, including the loss of pilot proficiency. Arriving at this decision was not easy, but the experience taught us important lessons about staying safe in the real world.

Safety is critical, but if we wanted to be perfectly safe, we would never fly. In fact, we wouldn't travel in our cars, play sports, or walk to the park. In all of these activities, there is a small chance that an accident can happen. Even though we know this, we seldom think twice about driving to work, playing basketball, or walking down the street. We all accept risk in order to live our lives.

And in the Air Force, we must accept some risk in order to accomplish our mission. The T-38 is a very safe airplane to fly. You have my word that if I learn of information to the contrary, we will stop flying immediately. In the meantime, we will accept the inherent risks of flying to accomplish the mission of producing pilots.

Accepting that risk, however, does not relieve us of the responsibility to be proactive. Just as we are tearing T-38s apart looking for other parts that could break, we should all look around our shops and seek out areas where our people are at risk.

When we find a dangerous situation, or one finds us, we must pause to consider our options. We should learn as much as we can and seek inputs from all levels. After taking time to think, commanders and supervisors should implement the safety measures that best minimize the risk to their people while allowing them to accomplish their mission. They should explain the problem and the plan of action to their people. After this, everyone should monitor the situation as they get back to work.

We can never drive risk to zero. However, we can continuously strive to make our workplaces and processes safer. As Airmen, we have come a long way. My grandfather used to tell us how he participated in too many funeral processions when he attended pilot training in 1919. Since then, Airmen have been tremendously successful in reducing risk while training and fighting in the air.

Now it is our turn.

Look into Their Eyes

18 August 2008—If we want the Air Force to be a family, we must do what a family does—care for one another.

At a recent conference for new squadron commanders, a commander's spouse asked me a great question: "What is the one thing we can do to make the most difference for our people?" My answer was simple. It's not a program or an event. You have to care for them. You will make mistakes as a leader, and sometimes you will encounter situations where there are no good answers, but if your people know that you care for them, they will overlook and forgive your faults. If you are sincere, they will respond by giving you their all.

So how do you show those around you that you care about them? Here's a simple way. Ask them how they are doing, and while you are listening, watch their eyes. Why? Effective leaders understand that the eyes are the window into the soul.

Many of us don't want to admit when we're having problems. We want to be strong, or we don't think our problems are big enough to talk about. When asked how we are doing, most of us will respond with the typical "I'm fine."

In the Air Force, we are fortunate—the vast majority of our folks are inherently honest. While we may say we're "fine," because that is the culturally acceptable thing to do, our eyes will not lie. If someone isn't fine, you will see it. And that's when you take the time to ask again, maybe in a slightly different way. You may have to ask several times. Take the time to do this. It's important.

For example, you may pass Airman Jones in the hallway and ask him how he is doing. Although he says "fine," he doesn't really look at you. This is your chance to make a difference. Don't miss it. "How is your family doing?" you ask. Airman Jones quickly answers, "They're OK," but he still doesn't look at you. Don't quit. Stop and look him in the eye and say, "You look like something's on your mind; are you sure you're OK?" Try to get him to talk, always looking at his eyes for important clues.

The fact is that we're not always OK. We all have issues in our lives such as relationships that turn sour, kids that aren't behaving at school, financial problems, or sick parents. These things weigh on our minds, and they can affect our performance. They can even lead us to contemplate irrational thoughts such as lashing out, leaving those we love, or taking our own lives. Unfortunately, we've had several people in the Air Force who have taken that road recently.

We are all leaders because we influence those around us. We can help make our Air Force a stronger family by showing each other that we care. Chances are that all of the people you work with have something in their lives that troubles them. Take the time to ask them how they are doing and watch their eyes when they answer.

We Are All Accountable

24 September 2008—Over the past few months, we've heard a lot about accountability in our Air Force. If you're a little unsure as to what people mean when they discuss accountability, you're not alone.

Over the years, the word "accountability" has been associated with high-profile failures, including shooting down our own helicopters in Iraq, bombing friendly troops in Afghanistan, and failing to keep positive control over nuclear components. Closely related to this, accountability has also been associated with specific sanctions, including loss of rank, forced retirements, and documented poor performance on fitness reports.

But focusing on only specific actions and sanctions misses the point. Accountability goes much deeper than that. Accountability is a matter of trust. Without accountability, we risk losing the trust of our fellow Airmen, our sister services, and the American people.

To be accountable is to be subject to the consequences of our choices. Whether we choose to do the right thing—to act with integrity, service, and excellence—or not, we have to be prepared to accept the consequences.

Even if others do not hold us responsible, we are all accountable—always. If we ever forget that as individual Airmen, we're headed down a very dangerous path. If we ever forget it as a service, we're headed toward extinction.

We are accountable for the choices we make in our personal lives. The vast majority of choices that get people in trouble involve alcohol, sex, drugs, and/or money. Each year, some of us make wrong choices in these areas and are held accountable. Sometimes, careers are ruined as a result. More importantly, a bad choice hurts the people we love—our families, friends, and fellow Airmen. If you have problems in these areas, go to someone you can trust and get help. If you know an Airman who is headed down a wrong path, help him or her before he or she makes a bad choice.

We are also accountable for the choices we make as military professionals. We must adhere to the standards we learned when we first received our training. When an Airman cuts corners by failing to follow tech order guidance or violating a flying directive, we must hold him or her accountable. When you see people doing the wrong thing, correct them. We must police each other, because if we don't small lapses will lead to bigger ones, and the entire Air Force family will eventually suffer.

Many of us in AETC are instructors. We teach and enforce the standards. It is also essential that we live by the standards. We must set the right example; otherwise, we lose our credibility. We all remember teachers whose attitude was "do as I say, not as I do." We cannot be like that. As we shape the future of our Air Force, we must hold ourselves to the highest standards of personal and professional conduct.

When you assume responsibility for others as a supervisor or commander, it is important to realize that you've taken a big leap in accountability. Simply put, you are accountable for the choices your people make. That is why you must lead by example. Your people need to see that you set high standards and live according to them. You must also enforce standards within your unit. You should correct deficiencies at the lowest level before they grow into something bigger. Remember, units with high standards have high morale. It's been that way throughout military history.

If we fail to hold ourselves accountable, we risk losing the trust that we have worked so hard to gain. Airmen will not trust a leader who does not consider himself or herself accountable for his or her actions. Just as importantly, the American people will not trust us with their sons and daughters, or their most destructive weapons, if we do not hold ourselves accountable. When things go wrong, our civilian authorities, our sister services, and the American people need to see that we take action to correct the problem and move forward, but assigning accountability is also critical for maintaining trust.

We do not want to return to a situation where the public doesn't trust us. I entered the Air Force during a time when public trust in the military was very low, and it was difficult on all of us.

In the years after Vietnam, we built trust by setting high standards and holding ourselves accountable for meeting those standards. It was the right thing to do, and it worked. Now, we must maintain these high standards. As we make personal and professional choices, we must remember that we are all accountable—always.

The Continuum of Training

3 November 2008—I believe we should work the problems of our boss's boss. I have found that if we see the bigger picture—and understand the larger context of our challenges—we will make better decisions. Since assuming command of AETC, I have been trying to understand where our challenges fit in the bigger picture.

My boss, of course, is chief of staff Gen Norton A. Schwartz, and his boss is Secretary Michael B. Donley. Together, they are responsible for organizing, training, and equipping the Air Force. They need AETC to provide Airmen of character and skill who can contribute on their first day in the larger Air Force. That is why we say that AETC develops Airmen today for tomorrow.

In the First Command, we recruit Airmen, give them their initial training, and send them to advanced schools. I call this process the continuum of training for our Airmen. While an Airman may go through several different training programs before attaining "mission ready" status, each of these programs should work together in a continuum—a coherent and consistent progression of training that leads to the ultimate goal of forging Airmen of character and skill.

Each of us has a role to play in this process. It is natural that we focus our efforts on making our individual portion of the continuum as good as it can be, but we cannot fall into the trap of viewing our individual roles in isolation. This is a team effort. If we understand where we fit into the continuum, we can make better decisions and produce better Airmen.

Much like a relay race, we run as hard as we can when it is our turn, then hand our Airmen off to the next set of instructors much like a runner hands the baton to the next teammate. While our portion is over, our race is not complete until the last runner carries the baton across the finish line. In AETC our race is not finished until we deliver the Airman to the gaining command. It takes each of us doing our part to make this happen.

In some ways, AETC is a factory that produces more than 200 different types of trained Airmen. We take raw material—the recruit—and change him or her into an Airman capable of defending the nation. The "assembly line" begins with the recruiter who finds and delivers the raw material to the factory.

Along the line, instructors mold and shape each Airman, then send him or her down the line to the next instructor. It is vital that the recruiter finds quality recruits, and each instructor must do his or her best to ensure an Airman with the right character and skill is sent to the next program. If they don't, future instructors will have to correct the mistake or, worse, take the Airman off the assembly line. Of course, our Airmen are much more important than objects on an assembly line, but this metaphor shows us how problems develop when we fail to ensure the quality of our people during the short time we have them.

While the quality of each individual Airman is important, producing the necessary quantity of Airmen is critical as well. We must deliver the right number of Airmen at the right time. If we don't, some career fields become dangerously undermanned, and the mission suffers. This is why we strive to create a "smooth flow" of Airmen through the training programs. Much like a pipeline, it is important to keep Airmen flowing through the training programs at the proper rate. Gaps and backups in the pipeline mean two things, and both are bad. First, our individual Airmen have to endure unnecessary breaks in training, and their skills inevitably atrophy.

Second, the pipeline cannot deliver the right flow of Airmen to the Air Force. This is why it is so important that our commanders and instructors manage the flow of Airmen through their individual training programs while ensuring each Airman meets the standards.

In AETC, we solve problems for the secretary and chief of staff of the Air Force. They are responsible for building a healthy Air Force, and they need a steady flow of trained Airmen. Our job is to recognize the big picture—that we conduct a continuum of training for each Airman—and make decisions accordingly. We are a team, and our job is not finished until we deliver Airmen of character and skill to their new commanders.

We produce Airmen of the highest quality, which is why our recruiters work so hard to find the right people and our instructors pour their hearts and souls into their students. At the same time, we produce the right quantity of Airmen to keep the Air Force healthy. I ask you to consider where you stand in the continuum of training. When you have a tough decision to make, use this larger perspective to make it. Work the problems of your boss's boss, and you will have few problems of your own. More importantly, our Air Force and our nation will be stronger when you do.

At War in Cyberspace

19 December 2008—"The stark reality is that the bad guys are winning, and our nation is at risk."[1] That's what retired Air Force lieutenant general Harry Raduege, Jr., wrote in an insightful article about cyberspace. As he describes our many challenges in cyberspace, General Raduege observes that "the list of concerns is growing and endless: rampant cybercrime, increasing identity theft, sophisticated social engineering techniques, relentless intrusions into government networks, and widespread vulnerabilities continuously exploited by a variety of entities ranging from criminal organizations and entrepreneurial hackers to well-resourced espionage actors."[2]

Over the last few weeks, we have focused on the security of our computer networks, and we have found that we have big challenges. The bottom line is that we are at war in cyberspace . . . today . . . all the time. Our enemies are attacking our network—the same network you use to send e-mails, share documents, and access the Internet. They are using stealth and surprise to insert malicious code into our network in order to gain intelligence. What is our enemy's intention? We don't know, but it's not friendly.

Rob Tappana, our command chief master sergeant, said something that caught my attention. He observed that if our front gate was under attack, we would do something about it. We would reinforce the guards with our security forces, convene the battle staff, increase patrols, and raise awareness levels throughout the base. Chief Tappana then pointed at the computer on a nearby desk and said, "We must realize that that's our front gate too." He is right. We need to think and act like warriors in cyberspace. That's where leadership is essential.

General Raduege describes four stages in our journey to secure cyberspace. The first stage is ignorance. We don't know what we don't know about cyberspace attacks. We are past that stage now. If you didn't know about our vulnerability in cyberspace, you do now.

The second stage is awareness. We now realize that we are at war in cyberspace, and we are vulnerable. We no longer take access to the network for granted; we realize that it can be taken away unless we take steps to defend it.

The third stage is actualization. We share a sense of urgency that we need to do something about the attacks on our network. We will learn more and more about cybersecurity. We will all work together to reduce our vulnerability and defend the network from attack.

The final stage is the "cyber mindset," where we think and act as warriors in cyberspace just as we do in air and space. We will train to protect ourselves and our networks from attack. We will all be "on patrol" as we look for new threats. Leaders at all levels will measure our vulnerability and direct defensive actions to counter the enemy.

To get to the fourth stage, we are going to have to work through a paradigm shift about security in cyberspace. Many of us (including me in the past) have taken the network for granted. We can't do that anymore. Every computer connected to the network is part of the battlespace. Every person that has access to the network is operating in a combat environment. Everyone must act responsibly, or it opens a hole in our defense.

As I've written before, I believe you are all leaders because you have influence over other people in your workplaces, your families, and your communities. It's going to take your leadership to help us make this paradigm shift. How do you lead others through change? You work through the stages of change faster than the people around you. So, as leaders, I ask that you move from awareness to actualization as quickly as possible. Talk to our experts, beginning with our communication professionals. Set the right example by following procedures and not taking shortcuts. Learn about and use the tools we have today. I promise that more tools are on the way.

I am working through the stages as fast as I can. We are improving the security of our computers at our headquarters. I have directed that no one is exempt from security measures, including me. If my computer has to restart while I'm in the middle of something, so be it. We must be willing to accept a moderate amount of mission degradation to secure ourselves against the enemy "at the gate."

General Raduege writes that despite the challenges facing us in cyberspace, he is optimistic that we are "on the verge of a new dawn for cybersecurity."[3] I am optimistic as well because we are fortunate to have you to help lead us through this change in our mind set. We are at war in cyberspace, and we will all need to apply our warrior skills to prevail. Fight's on!

Notes

1. Lt Gen Harry Raduege, Jr., "Evolving Cybersecurity Faces a New Dawn," *Signal Magazine*, December 2008, http://www.afcea.org/signal/articles/templates/Signal_Article_Template .asp?articleid=1784&zoneid=245.

2. Ibid.

3. Ibid.

Doing the Right Thing

20 January 2009—Last week, our nation was inspired by the actions of a brave pilot—an everyday American who reminded us of who we are and who we can be.

It just so happens that the pilot of US Airways Flight 1549, Chesley B. "Sully" Sullenberger, was a classmate of mine. We both graduated from the Air Force Academy in 1973. When I saw his picture on the news, I immediately looked him up in our 1973 yearbook, and there he was, looking sharp in his cadet uniform.

Sullenberger learned how to fly in our Air Force, and he served out his seven-year commitment as an officer and pilot. He then began a 29-year career as an airline pilot and safety expert. When you throw in his time as a cadet, he had more than 40 years of training, education, and experience to prepare him for the challenge he would face last week.

He prepared himself well. Like all Air Force pilots, Sullenberger spent hundreds of hours studying emergency procedures and practicing them in simulators. He obviously continued this practice as he transitioned to the airlines. One definition of integrity is doing the right thing when no one else is looking. Sullenberger made himself a better pilot by studying and practicing when no one else was paying a lot of attention. His foundation of knowledge and skill was strong because he put in the time and effort required to build it.

But preparation wasn't enough. When faced with a crisis, Sullenberger had to execute. He didn't panic. Instead he focused on what he had to do to save his plane and his passengers. Ditching a large aircraft is an incredibly difficult thing to do, but Sullenberger was able to do it safely. He executed his responsibilities with excellence.

Once the aircraft stopped in the cold waters of the Hudson River, Sullenberger continued to care for his passengers and crew. New York mayor Michael Bloomberg described how Sullenberger walked the aisle of the airplane twice to make sure everyone was out. In doing so, he put service to others before his own personal safety. In the middle of incredible stress and strain, he chose to do the right thing.

In media parlance, the story of Flight 1549 had "legs." Even as the historic inauguration approached, people remained fascinated with the incident, hanging on every detail as recounted by the passengers, ferrymen, and rescue specialists. Perhaps this can be explained by the sheer drama of the crash and the fact that it happened in our largest city.

I think there is something deeper here, however. I believe that in the face of all the negative news we have endured in recent months, we are looking for a hero—or in this case, a "Sully"—who will do the right thing in the face of adversity. Americans love heroes, especially "ordinary" people who do extraordinary things, because one of our core ideals is that everyday people can make a difference. On a very cold day in New York, Sully made a difference. He did it by living according to our core values of integrity, service, and excellence.

We didn't invent the core values in the Air Force. They came from the American people that we serve. Although the headlines may be filled with stories of fraud, greed, and waste, it is important to remember that there are millions of Americans who choose to live by these values. Whether it is the teacher who chooses to stay after class to help a troubled student or the policeman who chases the thief into the dark alley, many Americans choose to live according to integrity, service, and excellence.

The story of Sully Sullenberger reminds us of this. In these challenging times, it's good to remember what makes our country great.

To Sully, my old classmate: "Thanks for landing Flight 1549, walking down the aisle twice, and setting an example for us all."

Strengthening the Air Force Family

9 February 2009—"I also want to thank my brothers and sisters in the Air Force family."

If you have attended as many promotion, retirement, and award ceremonies as I have, you've heard these sentiments many times. We may not phrase it in exactly the same way, but the meaning is clear. When we reach certain milestones and take time to reflect, we recognize that the bond we share with others in the Air Force is stronger than for most business world coworkers. This is especially true when we factor in the emotions of deployments and combat. The term "brothers/sisters in arms" is no accident. As we live, train, sweat, and bleed together, these bonds grow so strong that the only language we have to describe our feelings for each other is the language of family—the Air Force family.

It would be a mistake to take these bonds for granted, however. If we don't respect and value each other, we risk breaking the family ties. This doesn't mean that you're always going to like everyone you meet in the Air Force, but if you grew up with brothers and/or sisters, you probably didn't always like them either. Building a strong Air Force family means that we each share a commitment to our fellow Airmen and treat them in ways that reflect this commitment.

I believe that we are all leaders because leadership is influence; we all have the ability to influence the people around us. I challenge you to be a leader in our family. You can influence others to build a stronger Air Force family by treating our fellow Airmen as family members. How? Consider the following thoughts:

A family laughs together. Our profession is serious business, but there is no reason that we can't have fun while we work together. When we smile and laugh with each other, we communicate a very powerful message: I enjoy being with you. Who doesn't want to feel like others enjoy their company? Laughing together goes a long way toward building a sense of family (as long as we are not laughing at someone's expense).

Having fun and playing together are behavior traits that we should extend to our natural families too. If your unit is not having parties, picnics, or play dates together with the families, go to your commander and volunteer to organize a fun outing or a get-together. I have found that the squadron, branch, division, or directorate that plays together stays together, especially when the times get tough.

A family cries together. When bad things happen to our family members, we are there for them. In our lives, all of us have issues such as aging parents, sick children, and financial difficulties. Moreover, our profession involves unforgiving activities such as flying or driving in convoys through a war zone; we will almost certainly know someone who is injured or killed while on duty. When these bad things happen, family members are there for each other.

For example, in AETC we have a squadron commander whose eight-year-old daughter was diagnosed with a cancerous brain tumor. Since word of this got out to the commander's Air Force family, the commander's personal family has been overwhelmed with support. Here's what they had to say when asked about how the Air Force family has helped:

> Since this whole ordeal started last August, our family has been blessed by every area of the Air Force family imaginable—AFROTC [Air Force Reserve Officer Training Corps] friends I haven't spoken with in 20 years, former F-117 drivers I didn't even know, civilian contractors and GS [general schedule] employees who are acquaintances at best, squadron and group friends, and lastly leadership all the way to the 4-star level. The Air Force family is a living, breathing entity that we are all a part of. You just don't get this kind of support outside of the Air Force or military!

This is not extraordinary—this is what families do, which leads to the next thought:

A family sticks together and takes care of each other. On the day that an Airman raises his or her hand to take the oath of service, he or she is part of the Air Force family. Airmen remain part of our family until we lay them to rest with a flag draped over their casket. During the time in between, we try our best to take care of each other by offering a warm welcome when a new person arrives on our base, by listening to someone who is lonely and far from home, by offering practical help to those left behind when their spouse is deployed, and in many other ways.

Last week, I had dinner with a senior Airman who had been injured in the war. As we talked, I found out that he had grown up in foster care. He had been separated from his siblings, so when he entered the Air Force, he was alone. I couldn't help but think to myself that we are the only family he has now. We must make sure that he gets the care he deserves because no one else will. In fact, we should go above and beyond to take special care of those who made big sacrifices in the line of duty.

We should also give special treatment to the natural families of those who gave their lives in service to the nation. I believe that when Airmen are killed or wounded, the units to which they were assigned should consider them "members in perpetuity." If they have been wounded, they should be invited to unit functions, and for those who have died, their next of kin should get a call from the unit on special days. It's the right thing to do.

You never know when you are going to make a difference in someone's life, so we should all live in a way that maximizes our ability to touch the lives of others. This means that we should have a healthy focus on others, not on ourselves. To paraphrase a wise person: we should not think less of ourselves; we should think of ourselves less.

Our profession is all about service to others. We serve our fellow Americans by keeping them safe and free. We serve our fellow Airmen by caring for them and their loved ones. To me, that is the essence of "service before self" and it truly sets us apart.

Leading in Lean Times

3 March 2009—"Be prepared." This old motto is still relevant today. As leaders, we must be prepared to face many kinds of potential challenges. Some challenges are so serious that, if they catch us by surprise, our mission and our people may suffer. I want to discuss one of those challenges with you now.

You don't need to do more than pick up a newspaper to know that our nation and our Air Force face challenging economic times in the months and years ahead.

Leading in lean times requires making tough choices, but it's important to realize that this is what leaders do. If you've ever heard me discuss leadership, you have heard me say that leaders must learn the art of balancing shortfalls because we never have enough money, manpower, or time. This is true in our personal lives as well as our professional positions.

We balance shortfalls of money by choosing to spend some now, saving some for later. We balance shortfalls of time by attending the school play instead of golfing. Supervisors balance shortfalls of manpower by prioritizing some jobs today and putting off others until tomorrow. This is normal because we will never have enough money, manpower, or time to do everything. We have to prioritize.

We often use tools to help us. A budget is a tool that helps us prioritize our spending. Another common tool is a schedule, which is really just a time budget. To prioritize jobs for our people, we use tools like staff meetings and "to do" lists. I trust you are using these tools already.

One tool I have found to be indispensible is the "unfunded requirements list." This list includes all of the projects and upgrades for your organization that are not in the budget. If you are a flight commander, this list may include new computers or furniture. If you are a wing commander, it might include a new hospital or parking lot. This list must be comprehensive and part of a multiyear plan for improvement. Most importantly, it must be in priority order. Your goal is to work down the items on the list one at a time, focusing on the top priority until you get the resources required before going to the next item.

You should be ready to execute the top priority at any moment since you never know when the resources will come. If the item is complex, such as a new building, it needs to be designed and ready to be contracted. Then, when your commander asks what you need, don't make the mistake of asking for many things at once. Focus on the top item on your wish list. Show your commander a vision (maybe a picture or model) along with the plan, explaining the requirement and logic behind it, and tell the exact dollar amount required to make your dream a reality. Remember this: money goes to winners, and winners do their homework.

All of these are things you should do whether resources are plentiful or not. While it is much more fun when you can knock many things off your list over the course of a year or two, in lean times you may go many months without getting a new item. This can be frustrating, but it highlights the importance of correctly prioritizing things.

To help with that, I recommend you go through this exercise. Think of it as a tool for leading in lean times.

Take a blank sheet of paper or a white board and write down all of the things your unit does. Begin with the mission statement and write down all of the tasks required to accomplish the mission. Additionally, write down the tasks that may not be captured in a mission statement. It's best to do this as a group exercise, and it is worth taking some time.

When you have reached the 80 percent solution on this list, draw three concentric circles. Label the inner circle "core," the middle circle "sustainable," and the outer circle "enhanced."

Now here is the big challenge. Match the tasks you have written down to the three circles. The core tasks are things you have to do to accomplish your mission. They are the foundation of what you do. (For example, if you teach pilots how to fly, you need to have some minimum number of sorties to accomplish this.)

Sustainable items are things that allow you to accomplish the mission with a high expectation for success and a comfort margin. In AETC the majority of our direct training courses have a mix of core and sustainable items in them. It is usually difficult to separate the two, but it is critical to do so.

The enhanced items are those that could be dropped without appreciable degradation to the mission, even if it might be painful for some.

When you have matched your tasks to these three circles, go back and examine your wish list. Is it really in priority order? If an enhanced item is your number one priority, then you should have taken care of all of the items that enable your core and sustainable tasks. If not, you need to reexamine your list.

In lean times, we must protect the core tasks. This means ruthlessly cutting the enhanced items first, then figuring out workarounds when sustainable items have to go. Sometimes we may have to implement a workaround that is uncomfortable, but we must in order to protect the mission and core tasks.

This has happened before. Our nation's military was cut to the bone in the years preceding World War II. When the war came, there was not enough equipment to train the large numbers of new recruits. Soldiers trained with wooden rifles and drove jeeps in maneuvers with signs reading "tank." I don't think we will see that again in our lifetime, but our forefathers left us a good example.

When tasked to mobilize for World War II, our military was able to call upon the skill and knowledge of superb military leaders such as Gen George Marshall, Gen Henry "Hap" Arnold, FADM Chester Nimitz, and Pres. Dwight D. Eisenhower. In lean times, these men spent long hours studying and thinking about their profession. They stayed in the service when they could have pursued more lucrative opportunities elsewhere. Their core task was to prepare for the day when their country would need them to build up the force and defend the nation. When the time came, they were prepared.

If we go through a lean period, our country is going to need men and women to do the same thing. Will you be one of those that lead us through the lean times and prepare for the future? I hope so.

Creating Candor

23 March 2009—If you ever have the chance to observe a flight debrief after a training sortie, you should jump at the opportunity. You will witness something special.

Everyone makes constructive comments in the debrief—positive and negative—regardless of his or her position or rank. If the flight lead did something that was incorrect or dangerous, the wingman is expected to say something about it. This is true even if the wingman is a lieutenant and the flight lead is a lieutenant colonel (or a lieutenant general). In the debrief, learning is more important than saving face.

In the flying business, it's imperative that the truth come out, even if negative, and the best ideas are heard. That is why frankness in the debrief is so important. Perfection is the standard, and although we will never get there, we must always strive for it. This is why we are tough on each other. We discuss our shortcomings and make constructive suggestions on how to correct them.

However, when the debrief is over and the door opens, we move forward as members of the same team. Should it be any different for our other operations? I don't think so, but it takes a strong leader to create this atmosphere of candor.

In order to encourage our people to voice their alternative ideas and criticisms, we have to be confident enough in our people to listen to negative feedback and dissenting opinions, find the best way forward, and then lead in a positive direction. We all like "warm fuzzies" when people agree with our ideas and give us positive feedback. We naturally dislike "cold pricklies" when people disagree and point out our shortcomings. As leaders, we have to be mature enough to deal with negative feedback without punishing the source; the best leaders encourage frank feedback, especially when it is negative.

We all have blind spots—areas where we think things are better than they are—and to correct these, we need to be aware of them. This means that we need to encourage dissenting opinions and negative feedback. We should ask open-ended questions. What are we missing? How can we do this better? What's the downside? What will other people say? When our people answer, we should welcome their inputs, even when those inputs don't cast our leadership in the best light. In the end, our time as leaders will be judged by the quality of our decisions and the accomplishments of our people. The personal price we pay in the short term for creating candor in our organizations is well worth the long-term professional and institutional benefits of hearing the best ideas and eradicating our blind spots.

As followers, we must work at creating candor as well. While the leader must set the tone for open communication, it is important that those of us who voice dissenting opinions or give negative feedback should do so in a way that it can have the most effect. We can't expect superhuman leaders. This means we should speak in a way that doesn't turn them off immediately.

Practically speaking, this means that we should avoid using superlatives and personalizing an idea or position. For example, which critique would be easier to accept? "Boss, your decision is really stupid," or "Boss, this decision could have bad consequences for our folks." Remember that your goal is to influence your boss to do the right thing. You don't want to close the line of communication before you begin.

When giving an alternative view or dissenting opinion, the more objective you are the more effective you can be. You should avoid emotional arguments. Instead, use facts and logic to back up your position. The more homework you do beforehand, the more likely you will win the argument.

In addition, when voicing your disagreement, be prepared to propose a solution or alternative path. This allows you to stay positive during a critique. If you can't come up with a solution, at least be honest about that up front.

If you are pointing out a blind spot to one of your leaders, strongly consider doing it in private. This is especially true if the issue is more personal in nature. It's much easier for a leader to listen to a criticism made in private; you want to avoid embarrassing your leader in public if at all possible.

We should also remember that the leader is ultimately responsible for the direction of the organization. If he or she decides to do something that you disagree with, you should voice your opinion but be ready to accept the leader's decision. Remember, most decisions are decided based on personal experiences and are not right versus wrong but right versus right. So long as the boss's decision isn't illegal or immoral, you should carry it out as though the idea were your own. That's the mark of a professional Airman.

Within our organizations, candor makes us stronger, and there are things we can do to create this openness while maintaining a sense of teamwork. As leaders, we should strive to set an atmosphere where dissenting opinions are welcomed. As followers, we should explain dissenting opinions with respect and objectivity. For both leaders and followers, the payoff will come as your organizations improve and grow. Consider it part of the price we pay to be the best.

Today's Airmen

13 April 2009—Recently, I had the distinct honor to attend the Airman's Coin Ceremony at Lackland AFB, Texas. It is always a privilege for me to meet the terrific men and women who train and are trained in what seems like a timeless setting.

That day, the crystal blue sky melted into the field of blue-suited trainees who proudly marched onto the parade field. They were surrounded by thousands of family and friends—all who had traveled to Lackland to witness something special. Everyone in attendance sat, buttons busting with pride, with eyes straining to catch a glimpse of their son, daughter, brother, sister, husband, wife, or friend. The American flag presided, waving prominently on top of the pole.

Like everyone else, I sat at the ceremony marveling at the 745 trainees ready to become Airmen in the world's greatest Air Force. This scene replays itself every week, year-round at Lackland. For trainees that afternoon, however, it was their day, and I felt it as soon as the first flight marched onto the pad. Everyone felt it—pride and eager anticipation were written all over their faces; these trainees knew they had accomplished something absolutely amazing.

I was especially proud of these Airmen. They decided to join something bigger than themselves and to defend our nation and its ideals. Within months, many of these Airmen will be sent forward into harm's way. I have no doubt that they will succeed. You see, our Airmen, noncommissioned officers (NCO), and senior NCOs are the finest in the world; it doesn't happen by accident. Our recruiters fill our ranks with members from all walks of life, and our training and education systems are second to none. We are a reflection of American society, and I wouldn't have it any other way.

Basic military training (BMT) is a terrific example of our Air Force's pursuit of excellence. The training builds upon the foundation influenced by mothers, fathers, grandparents, and teachers across the nation, emphasizing the Air Force core values: integrity first, service before self, and excellence in all we do. It transforms young Americans into members of the Air Force family, a motivated team of warrior Airmen.

Why is our enlisted force the best? In a single word: trust. When an NCO from security forces tells me that the base is secure, I know without a doubt that all is safe. Before flying, I always review the forms documenting maintenance actions on that aircraft. The senior NCO's signature at the bottom of the forms is all I need to see to have complete confidence in the safety of that airplane. I liken it to the cell phone commercial many of you have probably seen on television. Although there may be a single man or woman standing in front, he or she speaks with the voice of thousands standing behind. A successful team is one that works together, enabled and empowered by trust.

Where does the trust come from? It starts with our integrity, which is tested daily, and without which a team cannot operate successfully. Basic training reinforces it with the discipline, initiative, and competency essential to defend our nation and its ideals. Technical training continues the theme and is the next journey for these Airmen, where they will develop respective core competencies that fit into the overall Air Force machine. Later, these Airmen will become NCOs and senior NCOs, and the Air Force will depend on them to make difficult decisions—the "tough calls" that years of experience and training enable them to make. The Air Force machine relies on them and trusts them to make the right call.

All of us have a job to do, and no job is more important than another. One terrific example is TSgt Matt Slaydon. In October 2007, while leading an explosive ordnance disposal team to investigate a suspicious road sign in Iraq, Sergeant Slaydon sustained extensive injuries when a bomb exploded two feet away from him. As he later said during his Purple Heart ceremony, "It's a rare thing for a person to find a job and career that gave them great, great joy. Every day I loved coming to work, and after a short period of time, I gained a great sense of purpose from what I did. I know that those days are coming to an end for me . . . I think probably what I'll miss the most is this Air Force family and this great sense of purpose."

Sergeant Slaydon gets it. All tasks have purpose and, even the least glamorous, are mission essential. We must all follow his lead and embrace our function—our purpose.

On our Air Force team, everyone's ability to perform his or her function is what builds trust and makes the machine run so smoothly. Ultimately, we all share the same goal: the defense of our nation and its ideals. That's the common denominator, regardless of rank, where trust and mutual respect are paramount. At every base and in every shop and office, Air Force leadership—both officer and enlisted— consistently sets the example. We are all role models and always on the job. Our Airmen live up to these expectations every day.

Back at Lackland, the coin ceremony concluded with the Airman's Creed. All 745 spoke with a single voice—"I am an American Airman. I am a warrior. I have answered my nation's call." It was absolutely captivating, and the crowd hung on every word. As the newly coined Airmen finished the creed, their voices rose in unison for the last line, ". . . And I will not fail!"

The last words echoed across the field and stayed with me. I knew all of the new Airmen stood that afternoon wondering if they were ready, eager to be tested. In reality, they had just passed their first big test with flying colors. Other tests and challenges will follow, but these new Airmen will face their challenges as members of the Air Force team. I have unwavering trust in our team. Together, we will not fail!

Greeting Carmen

30 April 2009—If you haven't seen the AETC headquarters building, you're missing out. It is a grand, historic building that was built in the 1930s, nestled under age-old oak trees. Although initially used as an academic hall for new Air Force aviators, the building has had many uses over the years. Today it, along with sister buildings of the same era, houses members of the headquarters AETC staff. For those in the main building, standing every morning on the red-tiled sidewalk that leads to the front doors is Carmen.

Carmen is an important part of my morning routine. You see, each morning I park my car in front of the headquarters building and walk up that wide, red-tiled sidewalk to the front doors of the building. There she stands, working with a mop in hand, water pail nearby, and a bright smile that stretches from ear to ear. I always stop and talk with Carmen; she makes a difference in everything she touches.

Carmen is an unassuming, humble woman with a sparkling, energetic outlook that can make even the darkest day feel brighter. Through the years, she has worked to help support her family and has successfully raised two sons, now grown and on their own.

Although Carmen has held many different positions at military locations around San Antonio, she has made Randolph shine for the last eight years. Today, she isn't just responsible for the headquarters building. Carmen can be seen all over the base. You'll find her at the 99th Flying Training Squadron, the chapel, and even at the base fitness center. Carmen is everywhere, greeting dozens of people every day, and this base is better because of her.

Carmen works to ensure that her labor achieves the right effect—that everyone who drives past, visits, or works in the building feels a part of something special. The headquarters building routinely hosts foreign ministers of defense, air chiefs, and American civic and military leaders and represents the nearly 90,000 men and women worldwide that belong to AETC. The building is an integral part of the organization and is everyone's first impression at work every day. It all starts with Carmen's attention to detail.

Carmen's professionalism is evident all over the base, and it stems from pride. She never complains about her responsibilities and relishes the opportunity to make a difference. If she sees the flag in the front of the building rolled up by a gust of wind, she unfurls it. Dust on a ledge doesn't stand a chance. She's never idle, always taking the initiative to exceed expectations and set a higher standard. Everything she touches is better as a result.

You must realize that in Carmen's line of work, a job well done is rarely noticed or lauded. We, as a people, don't notice clean, but we do notice dirty. Carmen understands this and quietly creates a positive impact on the headquarters staff. Others instinctively and unknowingly follow her lead in their areas of responsibility and push for the same standard of excellence that Carmen sets daily. Such excellence becomes ingrained in the organization's culture. After all, people are far more likely to pick up a lone piece of trash on the floor than a floor littered with many. This adage goes for all things, not just trash.

What has impressed me most about Carmen, however, is her positive attitude. There is a lot to be said about someone who sees the world as being a "glass half full." True, we must guard such optimism with realism, but it is far easier (and more fun) to follow a positive, energetic leader than one who exudes negative gloom. Such a positive attitude is contagious to the entire organization and has a positive impact both up and down the chain of command. It is a key element of any successful team.

The one problem is that Carmen is so effective and efficient that her work begins to blend into the building. After awhile, it can be easy to forget the importance of her labors. I get accustomed to seeing her on the red-tiled walkway, and the routine becomes an expectation. I sometimes forget to appreciate her impact.

We must not forget that everyone in the organization makes a difference. No one person or position is of greater value than another; all are equal in the pursuit of excellence, and all contribute to the Air Force mission. We cannot afford to take anyone for granted—military, civilian, or contractor. The mission and our culture would suffer as a result.

All of us know people like Carmen, those at your base who quietly make a difference in people's lives. Take time to recognize and appreciate everyone. The next time you find yourself at headquarters AETC, take time to greet Carmen on the red-tiled sidewalk. She's made a difference in my life, and I know she'll make a difference in yours.

Develop Your Vision

2 June 2009—Try to imagine an adaptive training environment that sits inside a bare room. This environment can be manipulated to simulate any task, from simple to complex. With the flick of a switch or push of a button, the bare room transforms into a living, breathing, interactive experience. Sounds and smells abound; people appear and interact; and objects can be held and manipulated. Once the training is complete, the same switch or button disengages the system, making the entire simulation disappear, leaving the original stark, bare room.

In the "Star Trek" series, such an innovation was part of its daily routine. The "holodeck" permitted personnel aboard the Starship Enterprise to experience an interactive learning simulation. Imagine how such an innovation could help members of our Air Force. Not only would it save space, but it would also help manage risk, reduce training costs, and permit personalized learning programs built specifically for the individual. The holodeck would revolutionize all aspects of how we operate in the Air Force.

The holodeck is my vision of the perfect training and education aide. In fact, I wish every installation had hundreds of these interactive rooms throughout the base. The possibilities are endless. Sadly, I must temper my vision with reality and the realm of the possible. Although my vision may not be feasible today, it doesn't mean that I should give up. Our job is to make dreams come true each and every day. I know you all have similar dreams, visions that could benefit our Airmen both today and tomorrow. Such visions must be pursued—you should never, ever, ever give up.

In order to realize a vision, several things need to happen. First, you must align the vision with one of our core service functions. The closer to the core, the easier it will be to gain support and, eventually, resourcing. Next, take the vision and develop a strategy. Depending on your vision, the strategy may involve acquisition, implementation, execution, modification, or one of many other aspects. Let your strategy start at the 40 percent solution and then let it evolve to 80 percent and eventually to 98 percent. Realize that the process is continual—you will never get to 100 percent.

With the strategy in place, you can start socializing the vision. Socialization will also help your vision progress and grow roots through increased organizational support and understanding. The support will help you champion the concept for resourcing. After all, your vision must have resourcing in order to come true. Those resources will go to winners, not to losers; invest the time and energy to be a winner.

In life, and especially in the Air Force, priorities and personnel are always changing. Over time, your vision will need to adapt to the realities of change. It will require even greater persistence and objectivity. Giving your vision roots and aligning it with core functions will create something that can be handed off and sustained through change. The best ideas, sustained by hard work, can be carried forward by any leader.

You may also find yourself joining an organization and accepting someone else's vision. In this situation, evaluate that person's vision against current realities and resourcing priorities. If that person has done his or her homework, the project will be easy to move forward. If not, assess the vision to determine if it should move ahead or if its time has passed.

Last month, while visiting Fort Dix, New Jersey, and the Air Force Expeditionary Center, I came as close as I've ever been to a functioning holodeck. I watched in awe as deploying Airmen entered a series of rooms at the Medical Training Simulation Center. They fought through heavy smoke to reach bloodied bodies that littered the floor. Sirens wailed and explosions shook the room, all interrupting their efforts to save the simulated wounded.

Once their training was complete, instructors activated a switch that disengaged the simulation. In this situation, the switch did not make the entire interactive experience disappear. Although the smoke cleared and sirens stopped wailing, the "original stark, bare room" still held the medical training dummies. It was more than enough to get my heart racing.

My vision still needs some time to evolve and mature. This doesn't mean I'm going to give up; I simply need to work a little harder. Our Air Force needs you to champion your vision as well. Develop it along our service core functions and socialize it, let it grow roots, and evolve. Don't let your vision disappear like the end of a holodeck simulation exercise. Do your homework and the resources will follow. After all, it is your initiatives that fuel the positive change that makes our Air Force the finest in the world.

The Art of Objective Decision Making

29 June 2009—Making decisions is something we all do every day. Most decisions are made without much thought, almost unconsciously and, in many cases, automatically. Others, however, are decisions that involve time and thought and can impact more than just ourselves. These are the decisions where the process is an art—it defines who we are as leaders.

Saying this isn't a stretch. As leaders, we do things in order to create a desired effect. Making the "best" decision hits at the core of creating that effect and, in turn, is an essential aspect of being an effective leader. Now, these aren't decisions that involve "right versus wrong" or lying, cheating, or stealing—we must never compromise our integrity. In fact, most of these decisions involve "right versus right," and the decision may be different today than it was yesterday. This is what can make them so challenging. Let's take a moment to look at the elements involved in making the "best" decision.

Effective decisions require objectivity. The old adage "the more objective you are, the more effective you are" has never been more accurate or applicable than it is today. It can be tempting to look at decisions through the lens of a small straw. Effective leaders must step back and gain a much broader view; they must open their aperture. I've always advocated looking at issues and decisions from the viewpoint of your boss's boss. This approach helps to open the aperture and maintain objectivity.

In order to gain the broad, objective view, leaders must work to gather a complete picture of the situation. Some call this situational awareness; others call it a 360-degree view of the issue. In either case, that awareness involves considering all of the variables weighing into the decision, the competing interests involved, and the potential consequences. The potential consequences must include possible second- and third-order consequences. Tough calls like these can involve individuals, organizations, and issues beyond those initially thought. Weigh the consequences against unit missions and organizational goals. Investigate how the decision will move things forward in the near, mid, and long term. This will provide the context for the decision and, although it will involve a lot of work, will result in the broadest view of the entire process.

Tough decisions can be very emotional. Don't let emotion play into the decision-making process. Emotion only serves to cloud the issue and can potentially result in a decision where near-term happiness fades quickly into mid- and long-term unintended challenges. Leaders must look at decisions from the outside, unattached to the emotional influence from within. Leaders must rise above such distractions in order to maintain their objectivity.

Leaders use decision making to define reality. Decisions made within context and with the benefit of situational awareness will position future issues for success and establish tomorrow's realities for our subordinates, our boss, and, ultimately, our boss's boss. In the end, objectivity will ensure that decisions result in the desired effect and will keep you and your organization headed in the "best" direction.

It's All about Service

16 July 2009—SSgt Sarah Price worked diligently as a radar approach control (RAPCON) controller within the 71st Operations Group at Vance AFB, Oklahoma. If anyone had asked her what she did, her response would have been simple and quick: "I control aircraft."

No one would have argued the importance of her job, especially since it directly enables the student flying training that Vance conducts on a daily basis. Had you asked, Sergeant Price would have told you that her ability to make a difference in our Air Force was directly related to her capability to expertly control Vance's aircraft. Her perspective, however, was about to change.

On Sunday, 8 June, at one minute after midnight, the collective bargaining agreement between an Air Force contractor and its labor force at Vance expired, and student flying training stopped. Nearly 800 people went on strike—that's over 40 percent of the base's labor force! These were all key and essential people who not only ran aircraft maintenance operations, but also enabled most base support operations. Suddenly the base was without people to run the child development center, base supply system, environmental management programs, transportation, mail delivery, communication systems, civil engineering operations, and many other services the base's population depends on every day.

The leadership at Vance had to make some immediate changes to reallocate limited resources based on new priorities and realities. Services that had long been taken for granted were now in jeopardy. Student flying training was no longer the most important operation on the base. One minute after midnight on 8 June, Sergeant Price ceased working as a RAPCON controller and became the base's lodging detail noncommissioned officer in charge. When she returned to work, Sergeant Price began training in a brand new capacity to learn the intricacies of military lodging operations and even spent time learning how to handle hazardous waste! She and her team worked every day of the strike, including weekends. Lodging, a base service function with 100 percent occupancy at the outset of the strike, could not fail.

Being an Airman in the US Air Force is all about service. For many, when we start serving in the Air Force, this is simply something we do. As time passes, military service becomes central to who and what we are. This transition happens at different times for all of us, the sooner the better. When the Air Force is who you are, then you have internalized its core values. You'll spend the extra time to finish the job right. You'll stop and pick up the lone piece of trash along the road while jogging. You'll put the needs of others ahead of your own.

Is Sergeant Price's story unique? It certainly isn't in the 71st Flying Training Wing. The entire base population shifted responsibilities to keep the wing running. When the strike eventually ended more than two weeks later, the base was ready to return to its traditional allocation of responsibilities. Sergeant Price, her lodging detail teammates, and the rest of the wing returned to their normal duties.

Student flying training is once again a top priority for Vance AFB. Tranquility is defined by the sound of aircraft engines above. Vance's reallocation of responsibilities during the strike helped the base gain an important lesson in priorities. Base support services provide the foundation for Vance to conduct its primary mission: student flight training. This is just as applicable at every installation across the entire Air Force and not just at Vance AFB. Our daily base support activities can never be taken for granted. From Sergeant Price's perspective, "even the smallest jobs play their part in sustaining the mission."

Stories like Sergeant Price's happen every day across the Air Force: service-focused Airmen helping each other to get the mission accomplished, even if it means moving away from their comfort zone. In her wildest imagination, Sergeant Price never would have expected to have the opportunity to make such a positive difference in people's lives and in her organization while working for base lodging, not as a RAPCON controller. As Airmen we are all united by our commitment to integrity first, service before self, and excellence in all we do. Through our core values, Sergeant Price made a difference for Vance AFB.

If you ask Sergeant Price today what she does, her response, still simple and quick, sounds a little different—"I am an Airman." You see, serving in the Air Force is who she is. The sooner all of us follow her lead, embracing service and the other core values, the better our force will be.

Building a Winning Team

4 August 2009—On 4 July, I was fortunate enough to represent our Air Force at NASCAR's Coke Zero 400. I joined over 100,000 Americans, undeterred by the summer heat, at the Daytona International Speedway. The energy at the speedway was as thick as the humid air, and the excitement was contagious. Motor homes covered the infield, and racing fans were everywhere. This was my first NASCAR event, and I knew it would be a treat.

My first stop at the speedway was the Air Force recruiting stand, set in the middle of energy drink booths and race team merchandise trucks. Our stand was clearly a hit as race fans swarmed over the different displays. I watched in awe as members of the 333rd Recruiting Squadron managed the crowds with ease. The recruiters' enthusiastic smiles said it all—they were there to inspire. I was so proud to stand with them.

The crowd asked questions. They thanked everyone in Air Force blue for the service he or she provides every day. The recruiters reciprocated, engaging everyone with the Air Force story. They taught the public what the men and women of the Air Force do every day. You see, these recruiters were the first introduction many Americans would have to our Air Force; they weren't going to let any race fan leave with a bad impression.

The recruiters were also at the race to find new recruits to fill our ranks. Accessing more than 32,000 new Airmen each year doesn't happen by itself and isn't a process to be taken lightly. These new Airmen will be joining our team, enabling our mission for many years to come. We will depend on them to lead our Air Force through the next 35 years of challenges.

The recruiters looked for young, confident Americans ready for a challenge. I found out later that they found more than 700 potential Airmen that afternoon. I also learned that finding potential Airmen is just half the battle—only a handful of the 700 will eventually attend basic military training for various reasons. Before they get to BMT, it will be the recruiter's responsibility to invest significant time and effort educating them on opportunities within the Air Force and evaluating their potential to serve. It is the recruiter who will lead them through the upcoming months and set them up for success at both BMT and beyond. It is challenging work, but all of our recruiters volunteered for this duty and have a passion for telling America about our great Air Force.

From the recruiting stand, I transitioned to the speedway infield where NASCAR had set up a mobile stage on pit row. More than 100,000 race fans gathered to witness something special: a swearing-in ceremony for 65 new recruits. For the recruits, it was another step in their journey to BMT. They all raised their right hands and repeated as I recited the oath. The crowd roared in response as they finished, and each recruit's eyes beamed with pride. They knew they were joining a winning team.

NASCAR immediately transitioned pit row for the race, and the crowds moved toward their seats. When the race began, the crowd's attention turned from the booths and information stands to the battle on the oval giant. The recruiters didn't pause to enjoy the race. Instead, they attacked the displays, tearing them down and loading trucks that would drive to the next race.

While watching the event, I realized that the race teams competing on the speedway share many similarities with our Air Force. Our nation loves auto racing, drawn by the rare mix of competition, danger, and teamwork. It is this teamwork that ties the Air Force to NASCAR. The drivers, much like the operators in our service, stand in front as the face of the organization. Their success, however, is completely dependent on the hundreds of people that support from the wings. Like our operators, the NASCAR drivers would never make it to the track if not for the combined efforts of crew chiefs, engineers, logisticians, administrators, and many others both at the track and team shops.

However, one big difference between our Air Force and NASCAR drivers is how the teams are built. NASCAR builds a team that will compete for a season. It invests time, money, and manpower into training and race day execution—all with the ultimate goal of being the first to reach the checkered flag. There is nothing seasonal or static about our Air Force team. Without the ability of our recruiters to inspire the nation's finest to serve on a daily basis, our Air Force team would never be able to sustain its impressive record of excellence.

The race ended after a final lap crash sprung the eventual winner through the checkered flag. The crowd rose to its feet as the winning driver spun his wheels in jubilation. His pit crew stood tall, arms high in the air, congratulating each other on the team's victory. The Air Force achieves victories each and every day but rarely gets the chance to congratulate its recruiters. Take the time to thank them, for without these professionals and so many other support personnel like them, we would never even make it to the track.

Technological Change

31 August 2009—I am a digital immigrant. You see, in the summer of 1972, as a senior at the Air Force Academy, I spent $125 on a small personal computer. At roughly $650 in today's dollars, the small unit was able to do four things: add, subtract, multiply, and divide. It was a cutting-edge calculator. Although we were permitted to use it only while checking our work, essentially it was my introduction to the world of computing.

Today, we cannot accomplish our mission without technology and computing. Unlike me, those entering the Air Force today are digital natives. These natives don't remember a time when green military identification cards rarely left your wallet, the Military Personnel Flight wasn't virtual, and blackberries were just a seasonal fruit. This got me wondering. Has our leadership style adapted to take full advantage of the technology through the years? Has technology improved a leader's ability to make a difference?

Let's start by looking at how technology has changed the workplace. Beyond the most noticeable and tangible aspects—like e-mail, PowerPoint, and cell phones—I contend that technology has transformed the workplace in three main areas: collaboration, automation, and personal accessibility.

Collaboration includes our ability to network, collect, and share information. Getting the right information to the right people when they need it isn't always as easy as it sounds. After all, accurate information is a key element in making objective decisions, and objectivity is what keeps our organizations headed in the best direction. Today's challenge, however, is managing the sheer volume of available information. Technological advancements will only make this challenge greater in years to come.

By automation, I'm talking about technology's impact on the tasks we do every day. Historically, automation has been one of the enablers for doing "more with less." Our most expensive asset is our people. Technology gives us the ability to energize certain efficiencies by replacing manpower. Maintaining the balance of technology and manpower will continue to be a daily leadership challenge.

Accessibility applies to our ability to contact anyone, anywhere, anytime through voice and data communication. There are two key aspects of accessibility: (1) how leaders make themselves available to others and (2) how you, as a leader, take advantage of the availability of others. It is important that commanders, while making themselves available at all hours of the day, don't foster an environment where subordinates are afraid to get decisions from anywhere but the top. At the same time, leaders must guard against exploiting the availability of others, especially subordinates. Such exploitation will reinforce to subordinates that decisions can come from the top only.

Accessibility has also changed how we make ourselves available to others. Many commanders like to say that they have an "open-door policy." Don't fool yourself into thinking that issues will always walk through the open door. Leaders still need to escape the electronic accessibility, namely e-mail, and seek human interaction. A new Airman in the squadron isn't going to raise a concern by walking into a commander's office, but the Airman might if the commander is able to interact in his or her work environment. Leadership by walking around will always be a positive leadership principle.

I like to think that there are three kinds of people when dealing with technology: pessimists, optimists, and realists. The technology pessimists are those people who resist any change due to improved technologies. Technology optimists jump at the earliest opportunity to implement any technological advancement. The last category, the technology realist, makes up the lion's share of us all. The realist accepts that change is necessary and works to integrate improvements but doesn't continually search for and implement emerging technology.

Our organizations need all three technology types to run smoothly. It is necessary for each of us to understand what kind of technologist we, and those whom we work around, are. This is simply another medium where one size won't fit all. Leaders must adapt their style depending on whom they deal with and the nature of the task to be performed. The pessimist might not "hear" the things communicated electronically. By the same token, resist the temptation to send all correspondence electronically to the optimist, even though his or her response might be within seconds. Always push for the personal touch and realize that your approach will be different for each person.

In essence, leadership is the challenge of inspiring the people in an organization on a goal-oriented journey. Technology enables that journey, and we, as leaders, must successfully manage both the benefits and detriments of that evolution. Ultimately, leaders are still responsible for themselves, their people, and the results of their units. It's how they can make a difference in both the lives of their people and in the unit's mission. It is one thing technology will never change.

A Tale of Two Instructors

21 September 2009—Students and instructors primarily make up AETC. On the surface, the instructors simply teach certain skills so that students are ready for new challenges. In reality, they contribute so much more. Instructors make us better Airmen and continually raise our level of performance by enforcing the standards. They make a difference by tailoring their message and connecting with every student. I cannot tell you the number of times senior officers and NCOs have shared stories about an instructor who made a difference in their lives—I know you can think of instructors that had a positive impact in your life. I am no different. Let me tell you about two instructors that helped shape who I am today.

The first instructor who made a difference in my life was Capt Leonard J. "Chicken" Funderburk. He flew OV-10s in Vietnam and was awarded the Air Force Cross for heroism. He flew hard, played hard, and, at six foot five with a black belt in karate, was larger than life. Numerous stories about his heroic feats in Vietnam and phenomenal instruction in the T-37 "Tweet" were passed down from class to class. Even before my class left academics to start flying the T-37, we were awed by Chicken's reputation.

After graduation, I was assigned to "D Flight" in the 43rd Flying Training Squadron at Craig AFB, Alabama. Along with two other classmates, I sat at a table next to Chicken's. Every day, I had a front row seat to Chicken's postflight debriefings; it was a sight to behold. Chicken dissected every element of the training sortie and demanded that his students were well prepared and flew their best. His students, with nervous smiles trying to feign confidence, always started the debrief sitting straight up in their chairs. This posture never lasted long, for after two hours of continuous critique, smiles quickly vanished, and bodies eventually melted towards the floor. I was so thankful Chicken was not my instructor.

I flew training sorties with my assigned instructor and had some good days; other days I'd rather forget. Unfortunately, one of those not-so-good days was my "pre-solo" sortie. I "busted" the ride and wasn't cleared to solo like my other classmates. I was absolutely crushed. My flight commander decided that I needed a change and called me into his office. He told me he was shifting me to a new instructor. I'm sure he watched the color leave my face when he told me my new instructor would be Chicken.

I begged him not to do it, especially after just having busted a ride. I started to doubt that I would make it through the program. The next day I sat across from Chicken, mortified. I knew he could see right through my feigned smile. I tried to focus on my sortie as his deep voice stepped through the elements of the upcoming pre-solo mission. He told me one thing over and over again—"Always be hot and be high; never be low and be slow!" He must have said it 10 times. He took me out to the flight line and told me to climb into the T-37. Since I had busted the previous pre-solo ride, I knew this sortie really counted.

We took off, and he set me up first for a straight-in approach, followed by a single engine and then a no-flap landing. As I look back, each one of these approaches was average to slightly below average. After the last planned approach, Chicken turned to me and yelled, "Lorenz you are going to kill me. Put her on the deck!" With those words, I knew I was finished and probably going to wash out of pilot training. I landed, and he then told me to "shut down the number two engine." All of a sudden, I realized he was going to let me solo. I was elated. As Chicken stepped from the aircraft, he once again said, "Always be hot and be high; never be low and be slow."

I took off and had a very uneventful solo sortie. Chicken realized that I lacked a little confidence and just needed the right kind of instruction and motivation to succeed. Over the next few months, Chicken's demanding teaching style gave me the confidence not only to complete pilot training, but also to face subsequent challenges in both my professional and private lives. I have never forgotten him or how he made a difference in my life.

I encountered the second instructor who made a difference in my life much later in my career. In 1986 I was stationed at Castle AFB, California, and was selected to upgrade to instructor pilot in the KC-135. In order to upgrade, everyone had to complete a six-week program called Central Flight Instructor Course. It was a very demanding course that trained upgrading instructors how to teach aircraft systems and flight procedures. It emphasized the many ways students could unintentionally back into harrowing situations and helped instructors to correct the errors before everyone on board became another safety statistic. I didn't bat an eye when Capt Rusty Findley (now Lt Gen Rusty Findley, Air Mobility Command vice commander) and I were teamed with the most famous KC-135 Central Flight Instructor Course trainer in the fleet at the time—Lt Col Earl Orbin.

Colonel Orbin was famous for being straightforward, thorough, relentless, and demanding. We had both heard horror stories about how his level of instruction was challenging. Rusty and I had been flying the KC-135 for years; we were long on experience and confidence and looked forward to the course. After all, we knew the KC-135 and its systems inside and out. For us, the instructor course was going to be a breeze.

Through a series of Colonel Orbin's challenging training sorties, including grueling prebriefs and debriefs, one thing became clear: I was too overconfident in my existing abilities and systems knowledge. My overconfidence had led me to become complacent. During flight operations, much like other career fields, complacency can kill. It can lead one to overestimate his or her own abilities while not paying enough attention to the student's lack of ability.

I quickly changed my approach, increased my level of preparation, and arrived each day on top of my game. I left the course with the instructional skills I would need during each upcoming mission. Colonel Orbin was fair, firm, and demanding. He pushed Rusty and me—forced us both to grow as aviators and instructors. He reminded us that flying is an unforgiving business where everyone's limits vary from day to day, sortie to sortie. We needed to balance our own limits with those of the student. Since then I have learned to apply this lesson in other areas of my life as well. I think it has made me a better aviator, officer, husband, father, and friend.

Instructors like Captain Funderburk and Colonel Orbin make a difference every day and are the backbone of our Air Force's excellence. Although my instructors employed different techniques, they looked at me through a clear lens, saw where I needed improvement, and tailored their instruction specifically for me. When you have the opportunity, follow the lead of Chicken, Colonel Orbin, and all the instructors that have made a difference in your life. Take the time to make a positive impact in each of your student's lives—regardless of whether those students are found at work or in the community. It's what I strive to do each day, and it's the only way that our Air Force will remain the best in the world.

Cherish Your Spouse

20 October 2009—Just last week, while walking past the base chapel, I witnessed a scene that caused me to pause and reflect. I turned and watched as people, dressed in their Sunday best, flowed from the chapel doors, smiling and casually chatting. They slowly split into two lines, creating a path that led to a waiting limousine. The crowd stood and waited, fueling my anticipation. Suddenly, a photographer burst from the doors, then turned and captured a bride and groom as they ran outside. The crowd erupted with cheers. The bride—white gown flowing as she ran—paused to hug a friend. The groom immediately tugged at her hand, pulling her toward the waiting limousine. Without pause, they hopped in the limousine, and the crowd again cheered as they sped away.

I couldn't help but smile as I watched the newly married military couple start their new life together. It made me think about our spouses and our military families. The secretary of the Air Force and our chief of staff named 2009 as the "Year of the Air Force Family." In doing so, they hoped to bring more attention to the sacrifices our families endure and the service they provide our nation. I couldn't agree with them more; our families, especially our spouses, are the foundation that enables each of us to serve in the world's greatest Air Force.

I don't think anyone would argue the importance of having such a foundation. Our lives need balance, and our spouses help provide that stability. I like to use the analogy that such balance is similar to the spokes of a bicycle wheel. You see, a bicycle needs balanced spokes to provide a smooth ride. Our lives are no different. I think of the spokes as the different priorities in our lives. If one of the spokes—such as the relationship with your spouse, the needs of your children, or the responsibilities at work—gets slighted, the wheel no longer rolls the way it should. It might even get to the point where it stops rolling altogether.

We must balance each of our life's spokes very deliberately and carefully. When we are balancing shortfalls and managing a limited amount of time, money, and manpower, our spouses often are the ones who get shortchanged. We can't afford to let that happen and must always make time to tell our spouses how much we appreciate them. When you're tired from the challenges at work, take a deep breath, walk in the door with a smile, and tap your energy reserve to make a difference with the time that you have. It only takes a minute to let them know how much you care—a simple squeeze of the hand, rub on the shoulder, or a phone call during the day. Think about the things that make you feel appreciated and loved, do those things for them in return, and always strive to give more than you receive.

Maintaining the friendship, trust, and energy in a relationship isn't an easy thing to do—it's a full-time job. It's up to you to make it a fun job, for both you and your spouse. In a recent article, I talked about the danger of complacency in our professional lives. The same goes for our personal lives too. Many people confuse complacency with comfort. Although comfort can help build stability in a relationship, complacency can cause a relationship to drift apart. Never, ever take your spouse for granted.

Our spouses make significant sacrifices daily. There are countless stories of spouses who go above and beyond—stories of men and women who volunteer in the local community and pursue their own successful careers despite long days and the deployments of their military spouses. There are even more untold stories about spouses who quietly make a difference every day: the story of the wife who, after a long swing shift, returns home to wake her family, cooks everyone breakfast, and sends them all out the door before collapsing herself; the story of the husband who stays up all night taking care of sick children so that his wife can go to work rested and ready. Resist the temptation to become accustomed to such acts of sacrifice and kindness.

These tremendous examples are often interrupted by the "other" stories. We've all done "boneheaded" things—forgotten important occasions, not paid enough attention to our spouse's concerns, or tried to solve their challenges for them (instead of just listening sympathetically). Work hard to avoid these thoughtless acts in the first place. Be critical of yourself and the things you do. Your standards of excellence at work should be no different when at home. When you feel your spouse has neglected you in some manner, it is best to forgive without pretense. Put past grudges aside so that you can move forward together. After all, forgiveness is what you hope for after apologizing for those boneheaded things I just discussed.

As I turned to leave, the crowd had already forgiven the bride and groom's hasty departure and started to dissipate from the front steps of the chapel. The couple was starting their life together, as a military team. I thought of my spouse, Leslie. We made a commitment to each other more than 34 years ago. We knew that our lives would be better if spent together and have learned through the years to depend on each other in order to accomplish our goals.

For me, Leslie has been the key to keeping my wheel balanced. I've worked hard through the years to make each day with her better than the one before, to keep my wheel rolling smoothly. Our individual strength comes from the foundation that our spouses provide at home. By cherishing our spouses and making sure they know how much we appreciate them, our wheel can continue to cruise happily through life as well.

Spotting Disasters

23 November 2009—"I can hear that train coming down the tracks."

If you're like me, you've heard people use this analogy to describe an inbound issue or challenge. We all face daily challenges; they are nothing new. The challenges range in significance and in their ability to impact our organizations. Although the potential challenges do have unique characteristics, all have one thing in common: the sooner leaders can spot them, the more they can do to manage how the challenge will influence their organization.

In reality, it's pretty easy to know when a train is coming down the tracks. It is big, makes a lot of noise, and is accompanied by warning lights and bells. Trains typically run on a schedule, making it even easier to know when to either step to the side or hop on board. We rarely get the same notification from an impending crisis in the workplace. More often, it appears, seemingly from out of thin air, and immediately consumes more time than we have to give. Through frustrated, tired eyes, we wonder where the crisis came from in the first place. Even though we vow never to let it happen again, deep down we know that it's only a matter of time before the next one hits our organization by surprise.

Such an outlook is what helped create an entire school of thought called crisis management. We have crisis action teams, emergency response checklists, and other plans that describe how to effectively deal with the train that we never saw coming. These impacts can be hard to absorb and typically leave casualties behind. Wouldn't it be better to prepare for specific contingencies and not rely on generic crisis response checklists? Wouldn't it be better for the organization if a leader knew about the train long before it arrived?

So how does a leader get the schedule for inbound trains? In many cases, just getting out of the office and talking to the organization's members can help a leader identify potential issues and areas of risk. By the same token, if you are a member of an organization and know of an upcoming challenge, it is your responsibility to research and report it. Candor within an organization is critical to success; information must flow in all directions to maintain efficiency and effectiveness.

In addition to cultivating a culture of candor within an organization, a successful leader must be able to maintain objectivity to spot inbound trains. After all, allowing emotion to creep into a leader's perspective may provide short-term success but will eventually create mid- and long-term unintended challenges. Rising above the issues at hand makes it far easier to hear the potential challenges and competing interests before they arrive.

Candor and objectivity alone will probably help catch 90 percent of the issues before they impact an organization. In order to achieve 100 percent, a leader must work hard to avoid complacency. When things get quiet within an organization, it doesn't necessarily mean that everything is being handled successfully. In fact, the hair on the back of every leader's neck should start to stand up when things get quiet. After all, it probably means the leader isn't involved enough in the daily operation of the unit and that the first two elements, candor and objectivity, are being overlooked. This is the time to be even more aggressive about candor, information flow, and objectivity.

Leaders who work hard to enable candor, remain objective, and discourage complacency, get a unique opportunity to steer their organizations in the best direction when challenges or crises loom. As they identify the inbound trains, leaders can decide whether to maneuver clear or to hop on board. You see, each inbound train is an opportunity. It is a chance to fight for new resources—money and/or manpower—and to unify their team toward a common objective. Leaders should anticipate inbound trains as a means to improve their organizations.

Crisis action teams and emergency response checklists certainly aren't bad things. After all, no matter how hard you try, there will always be something that catches your organization by surprise. When you see a train coming down the tracks, don't just stand in front and brace for impact. Be ready to take full advantage of the opportunities it creates. Not only will you be more efficient and effective, you will ensure that your organization will continue in the best direction to achieve short-, mid-, and long-term objectives.

Jessica's Legacy

15 December 2009—There are certain times in our lives when a single moment or significant event causes us to pause and reflect. These moments can catch us after both happy times and sad—after accomplishments of our own or those of others. Sometimes they catch us off guard—by surprise. More often, though, these moments sit out in front of us, and we either run into their embrace or are drawn toward them despite struggles to avoid them.

This holiday season, I found myself at one of those moments. I was hosting a tour through the Center for the Intrepid (CFI) at Fort Sam Houston in San Antonio, Texas. The CFI is an amazing facility that helps rehabilitate military members who have suffered significant injury. I love walking through the CFI; it is a bright, airy building filled with hope. On the top floor of the circular building, there is a window-lined hallway with pictures of those injured Soldiers, Sailors, Airmen, and Marines whose lives were touched by the CFI team. It was there, looking at the large photos, that a particular pose caught my eye.

The photo took me back to last June to a memorial service for one of our Airmen who, at 24 years of age, left our ranks far too soon. SrA Jessica Tarver stared from the photo, a smile beaming from ear to ear. Her story is one of perseverance and strength. A rare infection that she contracted during her second tour in Iraq tragically led to two years of challenges that, along the way, took both of her legs and, eventually, her life.

Jessica's memorial ceremony at the CFI had seating for 75, but twice as many stood around the perimeter to attend. Such a crowd is one of the simplest and strongest compliments anyone can receive. She was an inspirational person, and I, along with so many others, am better for having known her.

During the ceremony, many people stood to talk and reflect on their special relationship with Jessica. Her squadron commander, Lt Col Raymond James, had flown to San Antonio from Hurlburt Field, Florida. Jessica's battle began right after he took command of the 1st Special Operations Helicopter Maintenance Squadron. In fact, he'd been on the job for only two weeks when Jessica first went into the hospital.

His words resonated, someone who had been forced to deal with a challenging situation from the very first days of command. Through

Jessica, Colonel James grew into the seasoned, well-respected leader that he is today. All of the members of the squadron and the Air Force at large benefited from Jessica's courage, inner strength, and perseverance.

One of her doctors stood to reflect on her memories of Jessica. While most double amputees work hard to walk in athletic shoes, Jessica told the doctors and physical therapists that she wanted to walk in six-inch heels. A tear fell from the doctor's eye while remembering the moment when Jessica strutted down the hall on four-inch stiletto heels with her prostheses. She had been an inspiration.

The others who flowed past the podium to tell their story and reflect on their relationship with Jessica shared a similar theme. Although their interactions varied, in each case they described a woman who challenged them to be better than before. She made a difference in their lives, and they were there to say "thank you." Through her example, Jessica left them wiser, stronger, and more able to handle future challenges. She was their wingman.

The caregivers from the CFI stood around the ceremony, embracing the sadness. These are selfless heroes who meet the unknown each day with a steadfast confidence and compassion. Their approach instills hope and enables otherwise impossible opportunities for their patients. They, too, make a difference in people's lives.

I could still feel the warmth of that embrace standing in the circular hallway last month, gazing at Jessica's portrait. She taught everyone so much, challenged all to grow, and strengthened our Air Force family. It is now our duty to pay this forward and push everyone to be better Airmen, teammates, and wingmen.

Such a message must never die. Standing in that hallway, I found myself feeling so thankful for having known Jessica Tarver and the way her smile could brighten any room. I also felt thankful for the members of the CFI team and all the good that they do. Lastly, I was then and am forever thankful for each of you, the service you provide our nation, and the difference you make every day. May we never forget the positive example and spirit of those Jessicas in our lives.

A Mentor's Influence

2 February 2010—Mentors touch our lives and help shape us into the people that we are today. We value mentorship in the Air Force and develop it in our subordinates while seeking it from our supervisors. One cannot have enough mentors, nor can one mentor enough. I've had many through the years, but one sticks out above the rest. This particular mentor touched my life in two important ways—separated by nearly 40 years.

While a cadet at the Air Force Academy, I struggled to keep my grades up. I was on the dean's "other list" six of eight semesters. In the end I managed to defeat my academic demons and graduate with a commission in 1973, but I certainly didn't do it alone. I owe my success, in large part, to my academic advisor and mentor Col Joe Henjum.

Colonel Henjum wasn't what I expected when I met him for the first time in 1971. To be honest, I don't think I knew what to expect. He had been awarded the Silver Star for heroism while flying helicopters in Vietnam. I quickly learned that Colonel Henjum was the kind of person who was easy to look up to and even easier to follow. When he took me and my academic worries under his wing, I was proud to be there. I knew that his guidance, combined with persistence and determination on my part, would lead me through the challenge. In the end, it most certainly did.

When I walked across the stage with the rest of the class of 1973, I strode with the confidence that Colonel Henjum had helped build within me. He had been a crucial part of my Academy experience and, in many ways, part of who I am today. I kept in touch with Colonel Henjum over the years, often thanking him for making a difference in my life. I never imagined that Colonel Henjum would impact me all over again, especially at this point in my career.

The second time Colonel Henjum touched my life began with tragic news. On 1 January of this year, Colonel Henjum passed away after a long illness. His son Mark asked if I would speak at his father's memorial service. I was touched by his request and spent hours trying to find the right words to convey how great a person had just left our earth. I wanted to make sure that everyone understood the lasting difference he made in the lives of others.

When it was my turn to speak, it came from my heart. I told the crowd about a man who dedicated his life to serving and helping others. When I finished, Mark rose to speak. While listening to Mark's story, I found Colonel Henjum leading me on another journey. I was touched and wanted to share the story with you.

A few months ago, Mark accompanied his father to the hospital, and they both knew what was about to happen. The doctor was going to tell Colonel Henjum that he only had three months left to live. It was an appointment they both were dreading. While riding up to the doctor's floor, Colonel Henjum greeted the janitor sharing the elevator with them. He complimented the janitor for keeping the building so clean. The janitor was shocked—no one had ever thanked him before. Colonel Henjum noticed the building and took the time to notice the janitor. It resonated with me. That janitor would never forget Colonel Henjum.

When getting off the elevator, Colonel Henjum introduced Mark to the receptionist. He told Mark about the receptionist's son who was a Marine and currently flying combat missions in Afghanistan. He reassured the receptionist that her son would come home safely; Marines are excellent pilots. Not only had Colonel Henjum met and talked with the receptionist before, but he also remembered her and took precious time to introduce his son. He even thought to reassure her fears with a son deployed to combat operations.

Now, think about it. Colonel Henjum was riding the elevator to find out that he didn't have much time left. Instead of lamenting his fate, he was concerned about others. That day, he made a difference in their lives. Almost 37 years after I had graduated from the Air Force Academy, Colonel Henjum was once again making a difference in my life.

I always like to tell people that they should strive for two things in life: making a difference in people's lives and leaving the campground better than they found it. Colonel Henjum certainly did that throughout his 75 years. He mentored me as a cadet at the Air Force Academy and once again just this last month. I couldn't ask for a better mentor and friend.

Go and thank those who have guided you through the years and take time to make a difference in the lives of those you mentor. Our Air Force is only as good as those of us who serve. Let's all work hard to make each of us a little better every day, just as Colonel Henjum did for me and many others.

A Dynamic Tradition

23 February 2010—Our Air Force has many traditions. Some we inherited from other services; others are more recent and will take time to fully develop. Traditions are positive things, deeply rooted in our heritage and pride. Traditions are things we don't easily give up.

One of our traditions, however, isn't often recognized as positive and doesn't get the applause it deserves. That tradition is one of our strongest and most resilient. You see, our Air Force is dynamic—always adapting to meet new missions and to counter new threats. With our world and its realities continually evolving around us, living in a culture of change is inevitable. This creates a level of uncertainty, and people generally don't like uncertainty. Such change, however, is vitally important and allows us to maintain our efficiency, effectiveness, and relevance.

So then, what is the best way for a leader to guide people through change? There are certainly many methods to do so, and each one depends on the type of change expected. In all cases, however, the principles that underlie the preparation for change are the same. Preparation builds confidence, helps a leader's organization be less fearful of approaching uncertainty, and ensures the organization is much more effective once change arrives.

This is where education and training come into play. We educate in order to prepare for uncertainty. Education helps us understand why the change is necessary. It also helps us objectively assess the environment and rationale necessitating the change. With objectivity, we can unemotionally assess the benefits and drawbacks of the different potential courses of action.

Education is a never-ending self-improvement process. The different levels are predicated to occur at specific spots in our careers—opening doors and creating opportunities. Because the Air Force lines up education programs with future levels of responsibility, it can be difficult to adequately catch up on education. Never pass up the opportunity to further your education.

While education helps us prepare for uncertainty, training programs are designed to prepare for certainty. After all, it's those things that we expect that fill our syllabi and lesson books. We train for them over and over until recognizing and reacting to them are second nature. This is one reason why we use checklists so often in the Air Force. They help lead us accurately through challenging times.

Through experience, our collective list of certainty grows. It shapes the evolution of our training programs. You see, when we react to a challenge, we create a certain result. Positive results reinforce the action and make us more confident. Although the positive result trains us to use the same response next time, it typically doesn't teach us to handle anything but the exact same challenge. When we make mistakes or experience negative results, we truly have an opportunity to learn. Even though it may not be as much fun to investigate our failures, we are more apt to critically assess the challenge and develop other, more successful, potential courses of action.

This is why our integrated safety programs, after-action teams, and lessons-learned archives are so valuable. They are an effort to take advantage of the experiences and mistakes of others and avoid having to learn the same lessons over and over again. In essence, such programs help us prepare for future uncertainty and help bridge our learning programs from the training arena into our education enterprise.

As a leader, you must ensure your people have the education necessary to prepare for uncertainty and the training to guide them through certainty. As an individual, you must aggressively pursue these opportunities to further develop yourself as well. Such preparation will instill the confidence necessary to embrace change.

Implementing new ideas in your organization can be challenging. It takes careful thought, skilled execution, and the full support of your team. It can also take time. It is always important to be evolutionary with change and not revolutionary. That way, your changes will have a much better chance to succeed over time.

Sometimes it is hard to take pride in a culture of continuous change. But within uncertainty is opportunity, and opportunity helps fuel growth. Today, we must all adapt to change more rapidly than ever before. It is one of our oldest and most important traditions, and one that I hope will never change.

The Solid Foundation

27 February 2010—Our Air Force has more than 175,000 civilian employees spread across the globe. In fact, they make up more than 25 percent of our authorized total force end strength. The civilian force fills an ever-increasing role in daily mission accomplishment, especially as we've experienced personnel reductions over the past 20 years and, many would argue, no decrease in operational requirements. In reality, we are busier than ever, and our civilian workforce makes it all possible.

Each of you knows many civilian employees. They are the glue that holds our Air Force together and the stability that our organizations rely on. Through the years, I've been fortunate enough to depend on the counsel and wisdom of hundreds of civilians. Time won't permit me to reflect upon all of them, but let me highlight three senior service civilians that made a positive difference in my life.

The first one I'll tell you about is Art Sarris. I first met Mr. Sarris when I was a captain at Wright-Patterson AFB, Ohio. A veteran of the Army Air Corps during World War II, Mr. Sarris began his civil service career in 1946 and worked his way through the logistics ranks until he became the senior civilian employee in Air Force Logistics Command in 1974.

Despite his significant responsibilities, Mr. Sarris took time to mentor me. He explained current issues and challenges and helped me see them through his eyes. Not only did I have an immediate respect for his tenured wisdom, but understanding his senior perspective early in my career proved invaluable throughout mine. Mr. Sarris also helped me gain a newfound appreciation for the thousands of civilians working at the air logistics centers across the country. After all, their efforts directly enabled the daily combat capability of our force then, just as they continue to do today.

I met many more amazing civilians during the next 30 years, but the next I'd like to discuss is Roger Blanchard. When I met him, he was the assistant deputy chief of staff for personnel at the Pentagon. Mr. Blanchard started his civil service career in 1973 as an intern at Kelly AFB, Texas, and diligently worked his way through the personnel ranks. When our paths crossed, I was the director of the Air Force Budget and marveled at how many sought his counsel, including service secretaries and chiefs of staff.

You see, Mr. Blanchard had no personal agenda, and his advice always reflected deep thought. He worked problems, not personalities. Not surprisingly, Mr. Blanchard was a quiet person. As a result, whenever he spoke, people turned their heads to listen. They knew that they were about to hear something thoughtful, relevant, and valuable. Through him, my respect for those personnelists throughout our force increased every day. After all, it's their expertise (in an often thankless field) that supports our greatest resource—all of us.

The last civilian I'll highlight is Bob Stuart. Bob was my deputy director of the Air Force budget during my most recent time at the Pentagon. When I got to the job, I was in need of some help. My Air Force experience up to that point focused mainly on aircraft operations, not the budget process. I was the fourth director he had worked for as a deputy. He had worked in finance at the Pentagon for more than 30 years, providing the stability the organization relied on every day.

Bob was always thinking ahead. In fact, it was his vast knowledge that helped guide the budget office. I've often thought that Bob's influence far exceeded what it would have been had he been the boss. In the end, Bob did as the others had done. He left me with a great respect for all those financial managers and an appreciation for their daily impact on the Air Force mission.

These three civilians are examples of the thousands who make up our Air Force team today. They are invaluable experts whose hard work and good, honest feedback help us to learn and improve. Although the advice may not always be something we want to hear, such counsel is what everyone should expect. After all, in most cases our civilian force has probably seen the pitfalls and potential second- and third-order consequences of our well-intentioned decisions before. Such vision only helps all of us make better-informed decisions for our organizations.

We can't be the finest Air Force in the world without our civil servants. They are the foundation that we rely on each day to do our jobs. Take time to appreciate their impact and thank them for making such a positive difference for our Air Force team.

Motivation

14 April 2010—These are challenging times for our Air Force. We have been engaged in combat operations since 1990 and are balancing limited resources against an aggressive operations tempo. We are once again adjusting to maintain our authorized end strength while juggling priorities within a leveling budget. Many of our aircraft are beyond expected service lives, and current operations are aging them even faster. Handling all these demands will be challenging—it will not be fun.

This is where leadership comes into play. Whether at work or at home, everyone has issues. As some issues are resolved, others are always waiting in line to take their places. The "pay me now or pay me later" mind-set is exhausting. It is up to each organization's leadership to set the tone, motivate the workplace, and create a sustainable culture of success. After all, we want our Airmen to invest themselves in our service and our mission.

So how can a leader attack such challenges and create sustainable excellence? We all know that it isn't easy to do. It will take dedication, objectivity, and a lot of patience and perseverance. Along the way, tough decisions will be required, and each will call for a tailored approach. In other words, leaders must adapt differently to each situation. Situational leadership is how we keep our organizations motivated and headed in the best direction.

We all have unique leadership styles. Some of us probably smile a little too much while others don't smile quite enough. We all fit somewhere along a leadership continuum, where the ends are defined by the extremes. Although you may feel most comfortable in one region of that continuum, realize that every leader will have to utilize approaches from the full range of the continuum in response to different challenges. A career brings many leadership challenges, and leaders must adapt to meet each one.

After all, some challenges will require leaders to soften their approaches. For example, someone in the organization may be directly affected by our end-strength reductions. Maybe the unit will suffer the loss of one of its members. Other situations will require a stern approach. This may be necessary when accountability and disciplinary challenges confront the organization or some of its personnel.

Effective leaders must be able to approach difficult decisions or situations with the entire continuum at their disposal.

In the end, leaders must approach a challenge with an eye toward crafting a solution to meet organizational needs. They should consciously select a leadership style or customized approach to create a certain effect. For most situations, mission accomplishment will be the effect—the end goal. However, before one can achieve such an effect, situational leadership must be used to motivate others toward success. After all, a motivated force can move mountains.

Motivation is an interesting concept. In some situations, motivation is more spontaneous and flows from the heart. In others, motivation is far from intrinsic and needs a little added emphasis from the top. I call it added emphasis because sometimes your organization won't be too thrilled with the changes after they're announced. It may feel like you are marching your team uphill and into the wind.

Leaders must look at each challenge, develop a plan, and push for success. As part of their plan, they must develop the motivation necessary to assist their organizations through the challenges. In the end, people don't quit their jobs (despite all the challenges we face every day)—they quit their bosses. The art of motivating organizations through challenges is one of the keys to any leader's success.

Today, more than ever before, we need intellectual leaders who value the power of thought and innovative approaches. After all, having leaders who think, assess challenges objectively, and motivate their teams to succeed is what makes us the formidable fighting force we are today.

Sustaining a Wingman Culture

11 May 2010—On 20 April, a 22-year-old man with a history of violence walked into a bookstore in Wichita Falls, Texas, and started shooting. He wounded four women, then drove to a bar and killed an employee outside before he drove home and took his own life.

This tragedy sounds like so many we hear about on the news every night. We've almost become desensitized to the horror and emotional aftermath, but this type of violence is something we cannot ignore, especially this event in Wichita Falls. You see, this time it wasn't just a news headline. It was an event that touched our Air Force family directly.

Wichita Falls is home to Sheppard AFB and to much of our Air Force's technical training. This particular bookstore offers a quiet environment that provides a peaceful and relaxing place to browse bestsellers. For some of the Airmen going through training, it offers a quiet place to do some evening studying. On that April night, three staff sergeants sat in that very store reviewing study materials for an exam the next morning. Two were former security forces members; one was a former F-16 crew chief. They were all at Sheppard to cross-train into the medical field. These Airmen were three of our best. They competed against thousands just for the chance to transition into aerospace medicine. That evening, the silence of their exam preparation was shattered by a man with a shotgun who barged into the bookstore yelling derogatory racial remarks.

His remarks shocked them, and the shooting that followed terrified everyone. They scattered and tried to protect themselves. It happened quickly, although the moment would be frozen forever in their minds. As suddenly as it began, the gunman was gone. The bookstore's peaceful silence, however, would not return. Four people had been shot, and two of them were Jade Henderson and Deondra Sauls—our staff sergeants. Police and emergency medical personnel were on the scene within minutes. Both sergeants were transported to a local emergency room and later to Dallas's Parkland Memorial Hospital for care. Thankfully, although their wounds were severe, Jade and Deondra will recover and return to training.

This is where the story ends for the local news media, but there are actually many lessons that can be learned from this tragedy. Although not wounded in the shooting, the third Airman, SSgt Tanya "Taye"

Jesser, avoided the gunfire by hiding under a desk near the shooter's feet. She watched his car drive away and yelled to the other victims that the gunman was gone. She was one of those who had the presence of mind to call 911, provide a description of the gunman, and request ambulances for the wounded.

Sergeant Jesser then followed the screams to different parts of the bookstore and provided care. She directed first responders to the wounded while applying pressure to slow the bleeding from one of her fellow Airmen. After emergency medical personnel were caring for the wounded, she contacted family members, reassuring them that all would be all right. Sergeant Jesser called a fellow student not at the scene and asked for help contacting Sheppard AFB, the security forces, and her first sergeant. After filing her report with the authorities, she gathered the personal belongings of her classmates and traveled to the local emergency room.

Sergeant Jesser didn't get back to her room that evening until almost 3 a.m. She woke before sunup and was in class at 7:15 a.m. Despite her lack of sleep and all that she had just been through, she took the exam as scheduled. Taye Jesser scored a 94 percent on the test.

The next day, I flew to Dallas to see our injured staff sergeants at the hospital. I wanted to make sure they understood that the Air Force family stood with them. Although Sergeant Henderson was in surgery, I was able to see Sergeant Sauls. I asked her if there was anything I could do—whether it was helping to notify friends, getting family members situated nearby, or even assisting with medical issues. Deondra Sauls looked me square in the eye and said, "Sir, don't let them take my training slot. I don't want to lose it." I was really touched. With everything that she'd been through, Deondra was most concerned about her future in the Air Force.

These three Airmen were among the many heroes of the evening. Jade and Deondra were worried about their classmates and their ability to complete training. Taye acted with a determined professionalism that facilitated immediate care and added stability to a horrific tragedy. When we talk about a wingman culture, these three Airmen personify such an ideal. They were concerned for others; they were selfless.

The lives of many were forever changed that evening. It's not only the individuals who were directly attacked—it's their friends and families too. In this disaster, it doesn't stop with the wounded. You see, the shooter also killed one individual that evening—even more tragic for his family and friends. The man killed was an Army veteran and the son of one of our civilian employees at Sheppard. He had his whole life ahead of him. Witnesses that evening said that his actions may have saved the lives of others.

No matter how hard we try to avoid or prevent it, this type of violence can occur at any time in almost any location. We must all do what we can to stay aware of how our family members and friends are doing. Look for times that they need a little more support or encouragement. Be there for them, even when they don't think that they need you. There are many heroes at Sheppard AFB and the surrounding community currently supporting those affected by this tragedy. Being a good wingman is something all of us need to try to do every day. Knowing that you'll be there for others should give you the comfort of knowing that others will be there for you, whether you think you need them or not.

The Study of Leadership

7 June 2010—Everyone has hobbies. Some people like to work in the yard, while others paint, fish, or travel. Hobbies are those things that entertain us when we need an escape, a chance to unwind. For me, I've always found leadership and its associated principles to be intriguing; studying leadership is my hobby.

I am drawn to leadership for many reasons. Most importantly, leadership is heroic to me. It is based on one person's ability to overcome interpersonal challenges and move a team of individuals toward a common goal and objective. It is all about moving the ball down the field. As military professionals, we all strive to do this every day.

Good leaders must be able to operate at three different interpersonal levels: a peer, a subordinate, and a supervisor. Most people focus only on the supervisory aspect of leadership, but the ability to work effectively within a peer group benefits all associated organizations. In fact, learning how peers handle their challenges can help leaders more effectively guide their people and organization. A leader's peer group can also help work challenges on his or her behalf. After all, having several people pushing a particular issue or solution makes the argument much more powerful and persuasive. Such symbiotic relationships help all organizations move forward toward achieving their goals and objectives.

To the leader's boss, those goals and objectives are called results. In our business, a leader is responsible for results, and results matter. A leader must also be flexible and adapt to his or her boss's likes and dislikes while keeping the boss informed. When mistakes are made, leaders must be open, honest, and transparent. Of course, they should tell their bosses about the good things, too, but shouldn't focus on them for too long. If something is important, they'll know; plus, good results are what they expect in the first place.

Still, the most important aspect of leadership involves those we lead. Leaders continually need to hear their input and opinion, realizing that their opinions may be fraught with bias and emotion. A leader's ability to stay objective will help screen out the bias and emotion to get the information needed. Remember that the people within the organization need to hear from the leader too. It is important that the feedback not favor any particular person, opinion, or organization, including his or her own.

Let the feedback act as a tool to mentor and shape future expectations. When listening to the challenges others face, don't try to solve it for them. Instead, ask what help they need in order to find a solution. Realize that 95 percent of the time they already have a solution in mind. If the leader always provides the solution, the team will cease looking for creative solutions and lose a certain degree of efficiency. In addition, the leader will not have as much time to spend working the issues that truly need his or her attention.

Your people need a guide who can provide overarching direction for the work they do every day. A leader's ability to know when to guide and when to stay back is invaluable. There is a fine line between a leader who is "hands on" and one who is micromanaging. After all, sometimes the best action is to do nothing at all. Trusting your people can be a very difficult thing to do. It might make things more difficult in the near term but will create a more efficient and effective team in the long run.

One word of caution—it can be very easy to lose perspective as a leader, to forget our own humility, and to gain a greater sense of self-importance. Never, ever lose sight of the people you lead. A leader must advocate for his or her people from behind the scenes, both personally and professionally. Your advocacy in support of the issues that you've asked them to work gives their effort more strength.

Being a good leader is a challenge. It requires each of us to understand the nuances of operating as a subordinate, peer, and supervisor. I read in order to better understand such challenges. In fact, I'm often reading two to three books at any single moment. To study leadership, I focus on biographies. The challenges we all face today are no different than those faced by the men and women who went before us. Learning how they handled challenges helps me be more effective with those I face every day. In many cases, it has helped me avoid the same pitfalls others found along the way.

As leaders, we all approach things differently. This is a good thing and is what makes it such an intriguing hobby to me. I encourage each of you to take time to study leadership. Not only will it make you better at what you do each day, but it also will further strengthen our great Air Force.

The Intellectual Resource

6 July 2010—Today, we are approaching nine years of sustained combat operations. Many could argue that our Air Force has been involved in continuous combat operations since the original Gulf War in 1991. Even more challenging, today's combat operations are being conducted while the rest of the nation fights its way through a recession, making resources extremely constrained. Such an environment demands a unique blend of innovation and intellect—looking for efficiencies at every corner in order to achieve our desired effect.

Sometimes it's easy to focus on resourcing and new weapon systems as the "innovation," the panacea for our challenges. Doing so, however, would cause us to overlook the most effective weapon at our disposal during such challenging times: the one between each of our ears. In many ways, investing in intellect—our ability to out-think the enemy—is the most cost-efficient way to prepare for future uncertainty and to combat a clever foe.

There are those that say there are three types of intellect, and we fit into a different category depending on the situation. There are those who come up with the innovative idea, those who understand the idea, and those who wouldn't know a good idea if it hit them in the face. Now, my description of the last group may seem a bit harsh. At times I'm sure we all feel like we're out of our element, but the times where you find yourself in the last category are also the times when you will have the best opportunity for self-improvement.

You see, we each bring a unique set of skills, experiences, and intellect to different situations. Although we would all like to be the "idea person," the individual who always has the innovative ideas, not every situation or challenge is suited to our intellectual talents. These are the times when we can be most critical of ourselves and take advantage of the opportunity to improve. In today's world, the easiest and quickest way to self-improve is to increase our individual levels of education. Remember, education is how we prepare ourselves for the uncertainty of tomorrow.

I know that increasing our education levels isn't always as easy as it sounds. Thankfully, the Air Force helps with one of the limited resources we balance every day: money. Scholarship and tuition assistance programs help pay for many advanced degrees and education programs.

Another limited resource that most people struggle with is time. Our challenge is making the time to find beneficial education programs and then completing them. After all, if it was easy, then time wouldn't be an issue, and everyone would have multiple degrees.

Think back five years ago and then 10 years ago. Were you any busier then than you are now? Chances are no. Do you think you will be any less busy five or 10 years from now? Again, probably not; the truth is you won't be any less busy or have any more time than you do right now.

Making a commitment to complete education and self-improvement programs may move other priorities to the side. When you're weighing the relative importance of each, remember that education and self-improvement are activities that will help you no matter where life takes you. If you decide to stay in the Air Force, it will help better serve the nation. If you decide to shift into another career outside the Air Force, higher levels of education and study will help translate into increased pay and responsibilities.

Either way, you win and are better prepared to successfully handle the challenges that life throws at you, especially when you least expect it. In the end, the better prepared that you are, the better the chance you could be the "idea person." Tomorrow's challenges will certainly be bigger than those we face today. Our Air Force—and our nation—needs you to better prepare now. Your investment in education and intellect is the best weapon to combat the uncertainty that tomorrow will bring. After all, we can't afford not to.

Professional Advocacy

3 August 2010—As a service member, I have fought for programs and resources throughout my career. In many cases, these battles were a matter of advocacy—my opportunity to fight for things I believed in. I began facing these challenging moments within days of my entry into military service. As a result, I have come to embrace several principles of professional advocacy that I want to share with you.

We all have personal beliefs and individual opinions. However, as service members we are expected to support professional positions. You must establish what the issues are that require your professional energy and passion. These issues will vary as your careers progress from junior- to senior-level leadership, especially in the face of diminishing resources and ever-increasing global challenges.

A Vision without Resources Is an Illusion

You must possess a vision. This is both a personal and professional expectation. We all have goals or beliefs that we want to see come to fruition for our unit and mission. These ideas vary in complexity and range in purpose from tactical to strategic. As we advocate for our beliefs, we must establish a priority list. This dynamic list should be rank ordered from most desired to least desired. When one idea is fulfilled, the next one on the list moves up in priority. However, sometimes an item at the top of the list may find its way to the bottom without ever receiving the necessary resources. This is a reality. We live in a time of limited resources, and we must learn to balance shortfalls where resources are the most constrained. However, the first step is to prepare your vision and then go after it.

Exercise Practicality

When advocating for your top priority, take a practical approach. Each time I am called upon to offer my opinion on a military matter, I mentally walk through a checklist of "do's" and "don'ts" that I have developed through previous experience and observation. First, do your homework. Understand what you are requesting, what resources you need (e.g., time, money, and manpower), and the risks associated with your position. Spend time researching your position thoroughly and reach out to functional experts for support as you organize your thoughts. It is also appropriate to know the positions contrary to your own. This means analyzing all sides of your argument. It is also imperative that you identify the end state. In other words, what is the desired effect you are seeking when offering your professional opinion?

Keep Your Ego in Check

In the battle of persuasion, inevitably your desired effect is not always achieved. In some cases, you must compromise for an alternative. In others cases, your opinion will be rejected entirely. Remember, you researched your position and know the facts, so now is not the time to let emotion enter into the equation. Emotion brings negative energy to the debate and takes an objective discussion and makes it personal. When it becomes personal, my experience tells me people stop listening. I think this is what great American military leader Gen Colin Powell meant when he adopted the following as one of his 10 personal rules: "Avoid having your ego so close to your position." General Powell writes that "when your position falls, your ego goes with it." Passion for your position is good. Emotion tied to ego is bad.

You Won't Achieve Everything You Advocate For

As professionals we have to recognize when our issues will not make the list or will be rejected. Sometimes this means knowing when to submit to a decision contrary to our position. Please understand I'm not talking about matters of principle. On those matters, it's important that we stand and fight for what we believe in. Ethical debates must be carefully examined as "right" versus "wrong"—we should always stand firm and fight for the right and against the wrong.

The larger point I am trying to make is an acceptance of "right" versus "right." When the final decision has been made by leadership, we each have a choice to make. As professionals we can accept the decision, salute smartly, and carry on as our leaders direct. Or we can lose our objectivity and resist the choice that was made. This moment is defining for us as professionals.

Leaders must cultivate a professional environment. If we center our conduct on each service's foundational core values, we will establish the very environment the American public expects and service members must follow. We have been called to great responsibility in defense of our nation and must remain rooted in the principles of our oath as we move our mission forward. Therefore, when the opportunity presents itself to offer your professional military opinion, I encourage you to be objective, do your homework, advocate for your vision, and always be professional. If you do this, I guarantee that over the years you will end up achieving more than you ever thought possible.

Spouse Wingmen

by Leslie Lorenz

19 August 2010—I recently met two young military wives. I was so happy to meet these bright, young, and eager new spouses as they and their husbands begin an exciting career in our wonderful Air Force. Randolph AFB is the first assignment for one of the couples. They are originally from the northeast and come from families with virtually no military connection. They've also just completed their first year of marriage. For the other couple, this is their second duty station. They previously had a wonderful experience at Columbus AFB, Mississippi, and have also been married a year. Both spouses had been here at Randolph for a short time. Unfortunately, their common experience was that no one had welcomed them yet. This made me sad.

I invited them to come to my house for a potluck salad luncheon with other spouses I've come to know since arriving at Randolph. Six spouses attended—my two new acquaintances and four others who were married to Airmen in training. The spouses of the trainees were busy, knew each other, and seemed happy and looking forward to their next assignment.

I opened the lunch by sharing my experience as a new Air Force wife 35 years ago. I differed from these military spouses in that I was an Air Force "brat"; therefore, I knew about the Air Force culture before jumping into it with Steve. I was also a bit older, having taught school for five years before we were married.

I told them that a couple of months into our marriage, I went through what we now call our "annulment period." Steve was so busy sitting alert, flying at odd hours of the day and night, and going to school on the weekends for his master's degree. I began to think it had been a mistake to get married. I missed my friends, my job, and my family, and I wanted to go home. Based upon my upbringing, it was assumed that I would simply adjust to the rigors of supporting my service member and everything he had to do. Over time, Steve and I worked through our initial struggles, and we've loved our Air Force life and all our assignments.

A version of this article was published by the AETC News Service. It was a part of the *Lorenz on Leadership* series.

A short time after our spouses' luncheon, one of my new acquaintances sent me a thank-you note and said she felt like I did 35 years ago. I realized that if these young spouses were feeling this way, probably others were too.

So as military spouses what can we do? How do we respond to this inadvertent neglect? First, I implore active-duty members to be aware of the sacrifices their wives and husbands make. In the scenario of the two spouses I recently met, I'm talking about the beginning of the Air Force life for new families. I observed two young people who love their active-duty spouses but have left everything that is familiar to start their life's adventure.

The staff sergeant or lieutenant is doing what he or she wanted to do—serving the Air Force. The servicemen go to work, meet people, learn new skills and, hopefully, step closer to their life goals. Meanwhile, their civilian spouses are in a new place, probably unemployed and seeking employment or perhaps enrolling in college. Worst of all is the lack of social support because they don't know anyone. The active-duty members should be aware and supportive while their spouse is making this transition. I would also submit that finding another couple in their situation can make the transition much easier. A retiree I once spoke to put it poignantly, "The spouse needs a wingman too."

This concept of wingmen transcends the active-duty force. I believe every member of the unit plays a role in supporting our spouses—especially commanders and supervisors. I ask you to please consider your own experience in your unit. Did you feel welcomed, cared for, and significant when you arrived? If the answer is no, think about what you can do. I understand the challenge with personal time constraints and operations tempo, but if your squadron, work area, or office isn't welcoming new people, consider volunteering to lead this effort.

We owe it to each other to welcome and support our Air Force family members. This commitment involves creativity, persistence, passion, and, most importantly, a heart for service to others. Are you willing to become a spouse's wingman?

Love Your People

30 August 2010—I have gained a wealth of knowledge during my career, but one point remains at the top of the list—love your people. Through "Lorenz on Leadership" articles and presentations, I have shared countless personal stories. While they always have different themes, one constant is the wonderful examples and lessons from people I have met. Our Airmen are priceless. They are what make our Air Force the most powerful in the world.

Loving your people is a personal tenet I fervently believe in and live to uphold each day. It is core to my passion and drive as a member of the armed forces and is an essential trait for leaders. Our military force's diverse makeup of service members and their families is a powerful reminder of the special charge we have been given as leaders in service to our country.

A humbling example of this is the story of Bradley and Sara Sullivan. Eighteen months ago Brad, an Air Force captain, was preparing for his first deployment as an F-16 pilot. Amid the flurry of predeployment activities, his family received two life-changing announcements. First, he and his wife were pregnant with their first child. Second, Sara was diagnosed with an aggressive form of breast cancer at the age of 28.

Following a number of difficult choices, Brad and Sara moved to San Antonio to begin her chemotherapy, which would allow Sara to stave off cancer and still allow normal growth of their baby. To their delight, the treatment went as planned. However, during the third trimester, the pregnancy became increasingly complicated due to the effects of the chemotherapy, and Sara was placed on bed rest. On 8 September 2009, Brad and Sara welcomed their daughter Chloe Grace into their family.

But their struggles were not over. Less than two weeks after Chloe was born, Brad and Sara were back in the hospital. Sara had suffered a massive stroke, thought to be a result of the physical ailments her body received from pregnancy and chemo. Within days of her return to Wilford Hall Medical Center in San Antonio, Sara was on life support and declared brain dead. She passed away shortly thereafter.

One of the many constants that continue to sustain Captain Sullivan is the community and network of unit leadership, friends, and family at Randolph AFB. You see, Brad and Sara were warmly welcomed into a unit that accepted them unconditionally and lovingly met every challenge with them as a family.

From the day of Sara's first hospitalization, their family was never alone as friends and family regularly visited. There was an even greater outpouring of support when Sara passed away. Now, as Chloe fast approaches her first birthday, Brad and his daughter are gifted daily with words of support, meals, and anything else required to help them walk in their new life. When difficult decisions had to be made after Sara's passing, Brad had a family liaison officer present or a member of unit leadership who was fully prepared to present him with all options for his family. All of this is a result of a culture of community—one that begins within our Air Force and reaches out to every member of our families.

Critical to loving your people is knowing them, not just what they do or their reputation at work but genuinely knowing them. As leaders and peers, we must invest the time to determine what moves and motivates those around us. It is essential that we know names of spouses and children. It is also imperative we understand the perspectives our people share. We must see the view individuals maintain of the world around them. This dictates an investment of time spent with them to hear their stories and life experiences. This stands to strengthen the bond you share with fellow Airmen and allows you to lead effectively.

Inevitably the investment we make in our people is returned. Often the return comes at a time of crisis, as in the story of Brad Sullivan. It is during this time that we owe it to those around us to focus centrally on what is in the best interest of the member affected.

Loving your Airmen is not a catch phrase, nor does it mean passively asking someone how his or her day is going. Rather, it is an active process, an investment on the part of leaders and fellow Airmen. You never know when you are going to make a difference, so never pass up an opportunity to reach out to those around you and invest in their lives. Trust me; it is an investment that will pay dividends for the rest of your life.

Ordinary People Becoming
Extraordinary Airmen

23 September 2010—During my 37 years in the Air Force, I have served with many great Airmen. Recently, the Air Force announced the retirement of five of our very best: Gen Howie Chandler, Gen Kevin Chilton, and Gen Roger Brady as well as CMSgt Pam Derrow and CMSgt Rob Tappana. Each one of these Airmen has selflessly served our nation in positions of great responsibility over many long years—in fact, together they total over 173 years of uniformed service!

These senior Airmen are leaders of the rarest form. Each ascended to the highest officer or enlisted rank in the Air Force, demonstrating a combination of exemplary character, personal intellect, exceptional work ethic, and an unwavering commitment to our nation. They began their lives in different places and under very different circumstances, but they have one thing in common: they exemplify how our Air Force affords ordinary people the opportunity to do extraordinary things.

General Chandler grew up in Missouri. He is the son of two hardworking parents. His mom invested her life as a housewife, caring for and raising him. His dad spent his entire career in radio and television broadcasting as a writer and producer. As the future general approached high school graduation, he chose to apply to only one college, believing strongly that he was destined to fly. He was accepted to the US Air Force Academy in 1970. Four years later, he was commissioned and began his rise among the fighter community. To date, he has completed more than 3,900 flying hours, predominately in advanced fighter platforms.

General Chilton spent his early years in Los Angeles, California. His father served in the Navy during World War II, then spent a lengthy career as a program manager with McDonnell Douglas. When this future combatant commander was just 12 years old, he experienced the exuberance of viewing a cockpit for the first time and putting his hands on the controls of an airplane. Although it was a small private airplane, he was fascinated by his surroundings. In fact, at one point in the flight, he turned to the pilot and asked, "Do you get paid to do this?" That flight was the beginning of his passion for aviation. In 1976 he graduated from the Air Force Academy with a degree in engineering and then spent the early years of his military career flying fighter aircraft. He attended the Air Force Test Pilot School and later, as an astronaut, piloted two space shuttle flights and commanded one.

General Brady grew up on an Oklahoma farm that his grandfather homesteaded in 1889. He is the son of two schoolteachers; his father also served in the Navy during World War II. As a young boy, this future Air Force leader was given big responsibilities in helping run the family business. His after-school chores often involved rounding up cattle in the evening while his dad and brother spent time at football practice. In 1964 he received an athletic scholarship to the University of Oklahoma. Four years later he graduated, was commissioned, and was given the opportunity to complete his master's degree. After a few years as an officer in the intelligence community and serving in Vietnam, he became a pilot.

CMSgt Derrow was the second of six children and grew up in Indiana. Her mother was fully employed raising the children, and her father was a factory worker. The future chief was working in a bank after graduating from high school when she and a friend decided to join the Air Force on the buddy system. After just the second week of basic military training, her friend left, but she persevered. She entered the Air Force in 1980 and spent her early career gaining expertise in a variety of communications assignments. An NCO Academy distinguished graduate, she earned numerous accolades during her years of service, including being named Federal Woman of the Year at MacDill AFB, Florida, in 1996. A leader of Airmen, she served as commandant of the Air Force Senior NCO Academy and as a command chief for nearly five years, culminating her career as the enlisted leader of a major command.

CMSgt Tappana was raised in the great state of Alaska. Early in life he developed a passion for outdoor activities. His inquisitive nature drew him to adventures as a hunter, fisherman, and explorer. His mom managed a doctor's office, and his dad was a schoolteacher. Each of them encouraged him to act on conviction and explore his surroundings. After visiting a recruiter, he entered the Air Force on a quest to see the world. He enlisted in 1979 and spent his early career as a traffic management specialist. He received countless honors and distinguished graduate recognitions throughout his career. Additionally, he spent nearly one-third of his career as a command chief. He was the senior enlisted leader for three wings, a numbered air force, and a major command.

Many may know these professional Airmen by their duties and rank. But remember, they were once young adults with a drive to serve and an unconquerable zeal for life, much like the young Airmen who make up the bulk of our force today. Anyone who knows these ordinary Airmen understands one principle is central to their lives: our service's core values. I have personally witnessed each one of these Airmen advocate and fight for what they believed was right for the defense of this great nation and for our Airmen and their families. They also each demonstrate skillful balance in their lives because they are guided by their faith, love for family, and true belief in the principles of freedom. Each leaves behind a legacy of public service, humble stewardship, and determined leadership.

While it is difficult to know how they, or any of us, will be remembered in the future, one thing is certain—we each have the opportunity to make a difference in the lives of others, to prepare and posture our Air Force for the challenges ahead, and to serve in awe of the wonderful nation we are sworn to protect.

Leaders Come in All Sizes

18 October 2010—Earlier this year, I wrote an article about the solid foundation on which our Air Force is so securely postured—our civilian force. Often, it is the continuity our civilian partners provide that enables our war fighters to project air, space, and cyberspace power when called upon. Without a doubt, our civilian force has direct impact on the lives of our total force team every day. One of those vital civilian components of the Air Force team is our world-class group of nonappropriated fund (NAF) employees.

NAF services encompass most, if not all, of the morale and welfare functions at our bases. These services vary widely and include golf courses, auto skills centers, base gymnasiums, child development programs, and libraries, just to name a few. Each of these programs is provided as a service to you and me, allowing us to relax during our off-duty time, care for our families, and take care of our health and personal well-being. These programs enable us to return to duty refreshed and focused on the mission.

They are, however, perishable entities. The unique and essential programs offered by NAF services are funded by our interest and business. In other words, if we don't support them, we face the reality of losing them. This brings me to a fundamental point regarding the critical importance of leadership in the ranks of our NAF partners. Leaders within NAF services have been called to serve and support Air Force members and their families. I have witnessed this firsthand as a member of the community at Randolph AFB.

Randolph is one of a few remaining installations that still operate separate enlisted and officers' clubs. The sole manager for both of those facilities is a NAF leader named Merilyn Gove. She is a tenacious leader and the fuel that energizes one of the Air Force's greatest base club systems.

What distinguishes Merilyn—besides being five-feet tall—and makes her unparalleled in her career field are several characteristics I have personally observed in my tenure as the AETC commander. First is her vision. Merilyn began her current role as general manager about two years ago. However, she has served within the Randolph club system for over 14 years. Her club team is now ranked no. 2 on the Air Force Consolidated Clubs Fiscal Sales list of 2009. She is driven by the goal of excellence and top performance in her craft and is fast approaching the no. 1 position. But her vision is not solely controlled by fiscal performance. Merilyn is motivated by a true concern for the people that she professionally supports—our Airmen. She passionately believes that what she does can, and will, have a profound effect on those around her. Such drive is personally motivating and is certainly permeating the Randolph community.

In addition, Merilyn daily demonstrates a genuine approach to servant leadership. It is not uncommon to see her fulfilling duties in a variety of positions within her own clubs. These include door greeter, server, cashier, and hostess. Her energy is contagious! In fact, I often wonder how she seems to be everywhere all at once. She firmly believes that there is no job too small and certainly no job insignificant to accomplishing her mission. This alone is one of the most powerful tools any leader possesses—leading by example. Merilyn demonstrates to her staff and customers that she is fully committed to them, her clubs, and the marvelous people she works with. This is evident in the exceptional staff and impeccable clubs they operate.

As military members we receive world-class benefits that we sometimes overlook. Throughout my years of service, I have come to greatly appreciate the variety of low-cost services that focus solely on caring for our Airmen and easing the stresses placed on our families. I am deeply indebted to our NAF civilian partners. They selflessly serve our military families so that we may continue serving our nation. And within the ranks of NAF employees are servant leaders like Merilyn Gove, those who believe passionately in their purpose and mission and have a direct impact on our Air Force mission.

Thank You

04 November 2010—This month I will officially retire and end my time as an active duty Airman in our beloved Air Force. Forty-one years ago, I stepped off of a bus at the Air Force Academy, although it feels like only yesterday. Every day since then has been a true joy—a chance to share adventures and tackle challenges with each of you.

When I stepped off that bus at the Academy, the Air Force was only 21 years old. To me, the Air Force didn't seem so young; it had always been there. I studied Air Force senior leaders of the era with awe. They had been through so much—World War II, Korea, Vietnam—and some even had old green Army Air Corps uniforms hanging in their closets behind the newer blue ones.

Now, I look at each of you with the same awe. The Airmen in today's Air Force have been given challenges like no other during this time of unprecedented regional conflict. And you all hit the ball out of the park each day; I couldn't be more proud or more impressed.

As I step away from active service in the long blue line, I want to leave you with three ideals. These are three unwritten rules I've approached with each assignment. They've helped me maintain a healthy perspective during the daily challenge of balancing limited time, money, and manpower, and they complement our Air Force core values of integrity first, service before self, and excellence in all we do. I hope that these three principles will help you just as they have aided me.

The first rule is critical—we must all cherish our families. Make sure you thank your spouse, children, and immediate family every chance you get; let them know how much you appreciate and love them. After all, our ability to serve the nation depends on their support and understanding. In many ways, their service to the nation is much more difficult than ours. High operations tempos, combined with our deployment culture, only add stress to everyone. Be understanding and invest time in their lives, no matter how busy or tired you may feel.

Next, we must try to always leave the campground better than we found it. I often tell people to pick two to three major issues to tackle during an assignment. Prioritize them one through three and integrate the challenges into a long-term vision. Now, it may take several people and more years than you anticipate for the beneficial effects to take hold. Be patient and let your organization get involved. After all, it always takes a team to truly improve the campground.

Last, we must attempt to daily make a difference in people's lives. Remember that each moment is important. Occasionally, you will find that people will come up to thank you for things you've done for them in the past. You may not have realized the significance of that moment, but it really made a difference in their lives. I am continually amazed at the emotions I experience when someone thanks me for words that I shared with them or something I did for their family many years ago. This only further reinforces the value of each moment and how important it truly is. Always speak and act with a purpose; always set the example.

I certainly hope that more often than not I have been able to leave fewer issues for others and help make our Air Force a better place today than it was yesterday. I hope that I've been able to make a positive difference in as many lives as possible, and that while treasuring my family, I've helped others to better appreciate theirs.

As a final thought, I want to express my deep thanks to the American public. It is humbling to know that our country entrusts us with its two most important treasures, the first being its sons and daughters. These young Americans serve gallantly in the face of adversity and are continually postured to carry out military operations across the globe. The Airmen in today's Air Force continue to persevere while challenged with a dynamic and evolving global environment. I can say with the utmost confidence that the future of our nation is bright because brave young people raise their hand to voluntarily serve each day.

Our fellow countrymen also have entrusted us with our national treasury. Public funds are the contribution and earnings of hardworking American families and, as Thomas Paine wrote more than 200 years ago, "ought to be touched with the most scrupulous conscientiousness of honor."[1] Knowing this fact has compelled me to honor the trust our fellow Americans have bestowed upon members of the US military. We must never, ever do anything to violate this sacred obligation.

Of course, the things that I've done through the last 41 years are, as I like to say, interesting but irrelevant. What is important are the things each of you will continue to do as servant leaders for our force long after I've hung my blue Air Force uniform in the closet. If you live the aforementioned ideals—cherishing your family, leaving the campground better than you found it, and making a difference in the lives of others—then tomorrow's Air Force will remain the premier air, space, and cyberspace fighting force in the world. Thank you for serving our great nation and thank you for making a difference in my life. Aim High—Fly, Fight, Win!

Note

1. Thomas Paine, *Rights of Man*, part II (London: J. S. Jordan, 1791), 331.

Preventing Violence

18 February 2011—Air Force leadership must collect isolated bits of information, like disparate points of light, to concentrate into a single beam focused on preventing violence.

The other night I was watching the evening news when the story of the 50-year-old wife of a deployed US service member stationed at US Central Command headquarters at MacDill AFB, Florida, was reported. The report stated the military spouse had been arrested for allegedly shooting and killing her two teenage children for "mouthing" back to her.

A TV cameraman filmed the mother being escorted by local police to the waiting patrol car. She was in a white jumper and stood stiff as a board while shaking like a leaf. As the camera focused on her face, her eyes were wide open, and she had a thousand-yard stare.

The reporter interviewed a couple of neighbors who talked about how nice a person the mother was and that she even shared in carpool duties while taking local children to sporting events. Later, it was reported that several weeks prior to the shootings, the daughter had called police telling them that her mother had hit her twice before. On another occasion, the mother had been in a car accident and had "shown signs of drug impairment."

This tragic story touched me greatly. In 1967 my family had similar issues. That year my father, an Air Force officer, went off to serve in combat in Vietnam for a year. No one died in my family while my dad went off to war, but he had to leave my mother, who had known medical and mental issues, and three children ages 15, 12, and eight.

In those days there was no e-mail, Twitter, Facebook, or Skype, so communication between service member and family was infrequent. To call to Vietnam from the States was very difficult and time consuming. A letter took almost three weeks to make a round trip to Vietnam. My mother was under the strain of taking care of our family, and she worried a lot about my dad in Vietnam. At times she took prescription drugs and self-medicated with lots of alcoholic beverages. Several times she made suicide gestures and took many of her frustrations out on us three children.

I was the oldest at 15, so many of the responsibilities of helping keep our household running and taking care of my younger siblings fell on my shoulders. I remember when my 70-year-old grandfather died; my grandmother and mother were so distraught that I had to go to the funeral home, pick out the casket, and make the funeral arrangements. My mother, now deceased, was a good person but was very ill. In those days there was some support for military members and their families but not like today. We are much better off as a military in taking care of our families, but as recent events have shown, we can and should do better.

During the last year of my active duty Air Force career, I had the privilege to serve on the DOD Independent Review into the 2009 Fort Hood shootings and then on the Air Force Follow-on Review (AFFOR) titled "Protecting the Force: Lessons from Fort Hood." We reviewed more than 20,000 pages of documents and surveyed more than 2,000 total-force military and civilian leaders. We ended up making 151 recommendations. (To view the complete AFFOR report, go to http://www.af.mil/shared/media/document/AFD-100930-060.pdf.)

While all of the recommendations in the AFFOR are important, one stands out above the rest: the importance of information sharing. With so many deployments in the last 10 years, internal violence shows many faces. These include radicalization, harassment, sexual assault, domestic and workplace violence, and suicide.

Today we have many outstanding people at various venues who are working these issues, like those at installation-level working groups, community action installation boards (CAIB), and threat working groups.

However, as more stress is put on the force, we have to do better. We have to be able to connect information from many different entities in a timely fashion to shine a light on those people who need help and assistance. We need a process that forces increased discussions among unit leaders, care providers, lawyers, chaplains, law enforcement officers, and intelligence personnel.

The AFFOR recommended establishing a new installation-level forum called the Status of Health and Airmen Resilience Exchange, which would be linked to the CAIB. This forum would better support local commanders and leaders in identifying those experiencing difficulties. We need better ways to build a family and the whole-person picture. We need a faster process to get the right information to the right person—commander, doctor, chaplain, and so forth—at the right time.

I realize that, even if we implemented all 151 recommendations of the AFFOR, we will not stop all violence. However, we must continue to improve our systems. If we stop just one violent act in our Air Force through these recommendations, then we will have been successful in building a better and safer service.

I can still picture the mother in Tampa, her two dead children, and the victims at Fort Hood, and I remember vividly my mother trying to hold it all together while my dad was in combat some 44 years ago. We owe it to our military members and families to do everything possible to ease the strain and the violence.

Widows and Children Left Behind

30 May 2011—On 27 April in Kabul, Afghanistan, eight US Air Force Airmen were shot and killed in the same action while serving our great nation and our Air Force. On that same day, three other Americans from our sister services also died in other actions around Afghanistan. These eight Airmen, two Soldiers, and one Marine who died that day in Afghanistan are American heroes who were doing their duty to protect our country while trying to help the Afghan people. They gave the ultimate sacrifice for all of us.

Those service members who gave their lives that one day in April were also individuals who left behind hundreds of people who loved and respected them. I was fortunate to know three of the eight Airmen. One was a member of the Academy class of 1999 when I was commandant at the Academy; one worked for me at Maxwell AFB, Alabama, in our commanders action group (CAG); and the third had been one of my instructor pilots while flying T-1s at Randolph AFB, Texas.

I was honored to attend memorial services for two of those who died that day: one at Langley AFB, Virginia, and the other in the Cadet Chapel at the Academy. Both ceremonies, which I am sure represented those held all over the country for the others killed that cold day in April, were professionally accomplished with tenderness. All the people who attended were sad but proud of the lives these great Airmen had led.

One of the most touching moments at one of the funerals was when the flag of our great nation was presented to the widow. She let out a cry of sadness that cut straight into everyone's heart, and then the missing man formation flew overhead with such a great roar. There was not a dry eye in the crowd.

At the receptions following the funerals, we all talked about these great Americans. We reminisced and told stories about these Airmen whose lives had ended so abruptly.

As the food was served after the Academy memorial, I noticed the little seven-year-old daughter of my former cadet who had grown up to fly F-16s and had become a husband and a father. His daughter, dressed in her Sunday best, was sitting all alone in the corner of the room playing with a small toy. She looked so small and all alone but was deeply engrossed in her game. She had read a beautiful prayer at the funeral service, and everyone in the chapel sat and listened to her read with great pride and sadness. As I watched her, I realized that she did not know how her whole life had changed because of the events of that cold, dark day halfway around the world in Afghanistan. She never again would be able to talk to her Daddy. He would never be able to tuck her into bed at night. Forevermore, for the rest of her life, when asked about her father, she will have to say that "he died fighting for us in Afghanistan."

At the other memorial service at Langley, I was honored to present the Purple Heart to the widow of my deputy CAG chief at Maxwell. He was somewhat older since he was enlisted before he became an officer. As I presented the medal to his widow, also an Air Force officer who has served overseas in harm's way, I saw before me her son who was born just a month before his father was killed. This young baby, who bears the name of his father, will never know or be held by the father who loved him very much. This young baby will know his dad only by the stories that others who knew his father will tell him in the future.

We all have a responsibility and duty to celebrate the lives of our Airmen, Soldiers, Sailors, Marines, and Coast Guardsmen who have paid the ultimate sacrifice for our nation. However, we also must remember that for every one of them we celebrate, they each left behind moms, dads, wives, husbands, and many, many children. In the years to come, please take the time to help those who are left behind. It is the ultimate way to remember those who have sacrificed so much for us all.

Leaders, Stress, and People of Faith

19 July 2011—Recently I was at a military base when two Air Force chaplains invited me to join them for lunch. We had a nice conversation on many subjects to include stories about leaders they had met over the years. One of the chaplains had just returned from his third tour in Afghanistan where he worked with the Army. The brigade he was assigned to was responsible for 18 forward operating bases (FOB). During his year-long tour, he experienced many great examples of leadership in very stressful combat situations. However, one example made a particularly lasting impression on him.

Late in his Afghanistan tour, he was scheduled to forward deploy to a FOB. As the troops were preparing to board the helicopters to a FOB that had recently been under attack, several Soldiers asked the chaplain if he could lead them in a prayer. A lieutenant colonel happened to be with the group, and the chaplain, who was a captain, thought as a common courtesy he would ask the senior officer for permission to say a prayer for the troops about to enter combat. The lieutenant colonel replied to the chaplain that "it would not be necessary" and walked away. The chaplain followed this senior officer's guidance and did not lead the men in a prayer.

This story touched me. The senior leader's own spiritual basis is irrelevant; he could have been Christian, Jewish, Muslim, Buddhist, atheist, or agnostic. It does not matter. What bothers me is that the leader appears to have ignored the spiritual needs of his troops. True leaders who have a mission to accomplish, especially in stressful situations, must take into account how different people under their command react during those stressful situations. They must get out of their own heads and into others. They must know that different people need different types of reassurance. For many of the people they lead, faith plays a large part in their lives and affects how they react in times of stress.

Our government recognizes the importance of free exercise of religion in the military as guaranteed by the US Constitution and so employs chaplains specifically to assist commanders in discharging their leadership duties. In fact, DOD Directive 1304.19, *Appointment of Chaplains*, states, "Within the military, commanders are required to provide comprehensive religious support to all authorized individuals within their areas of responsibility."

This leader lost a golden opportunity to show his troops that he cared so much about the mission and the people under his command that he respected their spiritual needs as they went into battle. The way he handled the situation left the chaplain, and I am sure the Soldiers who asked for the prayer, focused not on the mission at hand, but on his refusal to let a prayer be said. He also lost an opportunity to stand up for the constitution and our freedoms that the military fights so hard to protect.

To be truly effective leaders, we must respect the diverse people we lead. Each one of them is different, and that makes the units of our armed forces the strongest in the world today. We must be true to our own beliefs, but as leaders we also have a responsibility to the people we are sending in harm's way.

Life's Experiences: Luggage or Baggage?

28 November 2011—Recently, I was invited to speak at the US Air Force Academy's class of 2013 commitment night dinner. Commitment night is usually scheduled the day the third classmen (sophomores) return to the Academy and become second classmen (juniors).

Up to the very moment they begin their junior year academics, they can resign from the Academy and owe no commitment to the Air Force. However, once they start junior academic classes, they are committed for the next seven years—two as a cadet and five as an officer in the US military.

The night before the presentation, I could not sleep and tossed and turned thinking about what I was going to say to the 1,000 plus newly minted second classmen. At two a.m. I suddenly remembered an old suitcase that had many of my cadet papers in it. The suitcase was buried beneath piles of clothes in our closet and had not been opened in years. I got up and scrounged around in the closet until I found the 35-year-old beat-up brown suitcase. Unfortunately it was locked, and I had no idea where the keys were. The next morning I took the dilapidated suitcase to our building custodian, who was a retired chief master sergeant, and he had it opened in about five minutes. Chiefs continue to make things happen even in retirement!

As I rummaged through the suitcase and found many of my old cadet papers, waves of nostalgia came over me. In the suitcase were copies of my appointment to the Academy from 1969 and my silver-colored class nametag that was placed outside my cadet room and identified the rooms I lived in over the four years I was a cadet. There was a form 10 that I got for signing in late one Christmas and a copy of the cadet punishment I received for the infraction. There were also copies of all my grades, including the three F's I earned and the letters from the academic board giving me a second chance to graduate from the Academy. I also found a faded "Dear John" letter from an old girlfriend. Finally, in the bottom of the suitcase was my commission as a second lieutenant. The suitcase contained four years of my life's experiences, and not all of them were good.

That night, as I stood in front of the class of 2013 to give my presentation, I told them the story about the suitcase and dramatically opened it and displayed the contents in front of them. I explained that four years of mementos—both the good and the not so good—were in there. I told them how the contents of the suitcase had helped shape my entire life and that I could have used the contents as luggage that would help propel me on my life's journey or as baggage that would hold me back.

You see, life's experiences, like my bad grades, could have taught me that I was not as smart as the rest of my classmates and that I would always be behind. Instead, those momentary setbacks taught me to never give up and that lifelong learning can help you achieve just about anything, including becoming a university president.

The quality of your contributions to our armed forces and the nation as an officer, noncommissioned officer, or civilian is not determined so much by your individual successes or failures as it is by what you learn on the journey. It matters what you learn from both your good and bad life experiences; you should use them as a positive springboard into your incredible future. Your life experiences can either hold you back as baggage or help you along the journey as luggage. It is totally up to you.

Passing the Baton of Service
to the Next Generation

4 June 2012—On 7 May a friend and classmate, retired Lt Col Doug Dick, passed away after a six-year battle with cancer. Doug was commissioned in 1973 after graduating from the Air Force Academy and earned a master of business administration degree from UCLA.

Following pilot training at Craig AFB, Alabama, he flew KC-135s and later served as a staff officer at Wright-Patterson AFB, Ohio, and Andrews AFB, Maryland. After 20 years of service, he retired but continued to serve others as an elementary school teacher and principal in California.

During this entire time, Beverly, his wife of almost 39 years, was by his side, including those very tough six years Doug fought to stay alive. Bev was there during the radiation treatments, the chemotherapy, and the many surgeries.

The Dick family held the memorial service in California, where Doug had served as an elementary school principal for the last nine years. A week later a graveside service, attended by seven of his classmates, was held at the Air Force Academy cemetery. The chaplain said all the appropriate things, but it is hard to express the totality of a person's life that made such a difference in our Air Force and to thousands of young children as an elementary school teacher and principal. Also, it is hard to find the words that truly tell how he inspired all those around him during his six-year battle with the cancer.

The day of this solemn interment ceremony at the Academy was also the Academy class of 2013's ring dance day. My wife Leslie and I had been invited to attend the dance because our class of 1973 had been designated as 2013's legacy class. When Bev heard that Leslie and I were going to the 2013 ring dance that very night, she asked if she could also attend. She explained that almost 40 years ago to the day, she was Doug's date to attend our class's ring dance and that it represented the real beginning of their shared service in our Air Force.

That night, Leslie, Bev, and I got dressed up in our Sunday best and drove to the Academy to attend the class of 2013's big night—the night they were awarded their class rings. We arrived to the sight of

---

General Lorenz now serves as the US Air Force Academy Endowment president. A version of this article was published as "Passing the Baton to the Next Generation," *Academy Spirit*, 8 June 2012.

more than 2,000 cadets and their dates, eagerly anticipating a memorable evening. The women were young and beautiful and the men were young and handsome in their formal attire. The cadets had set up a World War II United Service Organization (USO) theme for the evening that included reenactors dressed in period uniforms, military jeeps, and trucks. The Air Force Academy band played nostalgic period songs, including tunes from Frank Sinatra.

After the rings were presented to the class and the cadets were beaming with pride, I watched Bev's reaction. From time to time, I could see tears well up in her eyes as she reflected back to her time as Doug's date some 40 years ago. You see, on that special evening long ago, Doug and Bev had their whole lives together ahead of them, just as the class of 2013 now has their lives ahead of them. We thought we were immortal back then, just as they do now. As the three of us watched the cadets and their dates get into the spirit of the evening and begin to dance, Bev reminisced about all the fun and challenges that Doug and she had during their 20 years together in the Air Force. She talked about all the places they had lived and the friends they had made.

As the evening came to a close, I too reflected on Doug and Bev and thought about our friendship and our service together. Over the years, we have been fortunate in so many ways. We had the honor to serve our nation and form lasting friendships.

I also thought about how fortunate the American public is. It is fortunate because there is a new generation represented by the class of 2013 who is continuing the great tradition of service to the nation. The class rings the cadets were awarded that night are a symbol of passing the baton of service from one generation of Airmen and spouses to another. I also know that not only the class of 2013, but all our men and women around the globe serving their country are taking that baton and will never let it drop. It made me feel good to know that the United States of America is in such good hands. When we left the dance, I thought Doug would have been proud.

PART 5

Other Articles

Linking Resource Allocation to Performance Management and Strategic Planning: An Air Force Challenge

Maj Gen Stephen R. Lorenz
Lt Col James A. Hubert
Maj Keith H. Maxwell

Abstract: As a service, the Air Force fights much better than it buys things. In fact, our service—the world's most powerful and capable air force—would probably fail quickly as a business corporation. We must do better, and this article raises some thought-provoking ideas about how to improve.

In late 2000, the service chiefs testified before Congress that the US military required upwards of $100 billion per year of additional spending (a 30 percent increase) to maintain readiness and modernize the force. But the recent tax cut, a slow economy, and spending increases needed for nonmilitary priorities make a 30 percent increase in defense spending unlikely. Without the needed funds, the military will face many difficult decisions concerning allocation of the remaining resources. The question is and always has been—what is the best way to allocate those limited resources?

The approach to allocating resources throughout the DOD at the beginning of the twenty-first century has several deficiencies. It doesn't provide connections from where we are (performance), to where we want to go (strategy), and to how we get there (resources). In addition, the process identifies shortfalls but not the sources to pay for them.

It rewards advocates who are the most adept at articulating increases in spending but sometimes punishes programs that can produce savings. Even worse, it lacks fundamental measures of value on which to base decisions. Eliminating these deficiencies may not solve the shortfall in resources, but it can ensure that we spend the money we have more wisely.

A version of this article was published as "Linking Resource Allocation to Performance Management and Strategic Planning: An Air Force Challenge," *Aerospace Power Journal* 25, no. 4 (Winter 2001): 34–45. It was written before 11 September 2001 when General Lorenz was the USAFE/XP and resources were very tight, just as today.

The key to enabling Air Force leaders to make better resource decisions lies in implementing three major changes in the way we do business. These three management functions must work in unison to ensure consistent direction. First, we must link resource allocation to performance management and strategic planning. Second, we need a process that is simple, transparent, and reproducible. It must be simple enough to be implemented quickly and improved upon; it must be transparent to identify the trade-offs and provide incentives for cost reduction; and it must be reproducible through a structured planning framework that relates capability to cost. Third, we must deliver the best value to the war fighter over time and with the resources available. This requires measuring Air Force capabilities and relating them to resources and operational effectiveness for the near-, mid-, and long terms.

Such changes are within reach; however, getting there requires a cultural change. The Air Force management processes currently in place provide little incentive to reduce costs and only limited accountability for those costs. Gen Gregory S. Martin, commander of US Air Forces in Europe (USAFE), recently observed that "the only way we're going to get anywhere in the Air Force today is to develop the tools and performance measures which will allow our people to have control and accountability for their resource and mission performance. And then we can push decisions hard and fast to the lowest level possible. . . . That's the only way we'll really make major progress in the future."[1]

The Air Force has recognized the need for change and is making the transition. Under the leadership of F. Whitten Peters, the former secretary of the Air Force, and Gen Michael E. Ryan, the former chief of staff, Headquarters Air Force created a team to reengineer the Air Force Resource Allocation Process (AFRAP). Led by Maj Gen Danny A. Hogan, the AFRAP team recommended a capabilities-based process for allocating resources.[2] As a result, Headquarters Air Force chose a new approach for building the budget for fiscal year 2003 (FY 03) as an initial step to implementing the AFRAP recommendations. Each major command received a top-line dollar amount along with the direction to present a balanced, capabilities-based input to the amended Program Objective Memorandum (POM) for FY 03.

The USAFE team responded by developing a resource allocation model (RAM) that produced a balanced program and at the same time provided tremendous insight into the command's capabilities.

The purpose here is not to wave the USAFE flag but to use its experience as a case study. The USAFE RAM not only works for an operations and maintenance command, but also offers promise towards improving resource allocation for the entire Air Force.

We're on a Journey

Throughout history, military spending has been based on available resources that the citizens of a country were willing to spend in peacetime and war. At the macro level, we won the Cold War by engaging in a long-term expenditure of resources while maintaining a large standing military. Today, with our vision of global vigilance, reach, and power, significant technological advantages have changed this equation. Vigilance has progressed from scouts and spies taking days or weeks to provide information to satellites and remotely piloted aircraft producing results in minutes. Reach has progressed from the walking pace of horse-drawn wagons to moving millions of ton-miles per day (thousands of tons halfway around the world every day). Technological advances in precision and stealth have significantly changed the nature of power in battle from using numerous, large munitions to destroy a target to using fewer, more precise weapons to achieve desired effects. Beginning with Operation Desert Storm and progressing further during the air war over Serbia under the leadership of Gen John P. Jumper, then the commander of USAFE, the goal has now become "effects-based" operations.[3] Technology has enabled us to pick and choose which of the enemy's centers of gravity to affect and to strike them with crippling speed.

In the past, military spending drove the pace of technology. Militaries were both technology and resource limited. Over time, technology became profitable enough so that the private sector now takes the lead in many areas. As a result, we are faced with more technological choices than we can pursue with our available resources. Being resource constrained puts a premium on planning that is compounded by a rapid increase in system complexity. Automation and computers have resulted in systems of systems interdependent with other systems of systems. For example, satellite navigation, radio communications, precision weapons, and aircraft form complex systems of systems used to perform many attack missions.

In the late 1950s and early 1960s, Secretary of Defense Robert Mc-Namara and his "whiz kids" responded to the increasing difficulty in allocating resources with the Planning, Programming, and Budgeting System (PPBS).[4] Until that time, each department received fiscal spending limits along with direction on how to spend the resources. Today, the major force programs and associated program elements provide the PPBS framework. Each program element is programmed with funds for five to six years in advance of the current budget. DOD went from little involvement in how the services spent their resources to detailed programmatic insight.

At the time of PPBS development, the military planning system was considered the best ever. But we have since realized that military planning has two broad categories: operational planning and force planning.[5] Although military operational planning and the associated logistical planning have proven extremely capable, force planning has never been highly developed. Even today, the Quadrennial Defense Review (QDR) is part of an informal process used by the DOD to establish force structure.[6]

In 1993 Congress passed the Government Performance and Results Act, which requires government agencies to take responsibility for effectively allocating and expending resources through strategic planning and performance management.[7] It also spawned the National Partnership for Reinventing Government, which, over the last eight years, has fostered numerous studies, experiments, and reforms in government planning and management.[8] In response to the Government Performance and Results Act, the DOD published its performance plan and captured its strategic plan through the QDR. Until recently, DOD and Air Force reforms have failed to address the key deficiencies in the PPBS process.

In 2000 the AFRAP process reengineering team developed a capabilities-based approach for resource allocation, reviewing PPBS and the related processes in place to establish requirements, make acquisition decisions, manage execution, and perform analysis. The recommendations included significant enhancements to the planning portion of PPBS by combining programming and budgeting and adding execution management.[9]

The fundamental key to implementing AFRAP is development of an Air Force capabilities framework to tie the elements of resource allocation together and serve as a basis for making decisions. Once the capability relationships are established, the AFRAP solution develops numerical capability objectives and projects them over time. These objectives are validated through the rest of the process by planning the capability solutions and associated resources over an 18-year time frame. Finally, accounting and performance-management systems provide feedback directly to the capabilities assessment in order to judge progress.

But We Have Miles to Go

The DOD and the Air Force have transformed in many ways recently, but, until AFRAP, neither adequately addressed the overarching issue of affordability. As a result, we still don't really know whether we are spending our resources effectively and efficiently. A recent acquisition-reform effort first identified affordability as the missing link. In 1995 Dr. Paul G. Kaminski, undersecretary of defense for acquisition and technology, created an initiative called "Cost as an Independent Variable."[10] A team, formed with the objective of treating cost as importantly as performance, concluded that the key lay in establishing "affordable cost targets" for acquisition programs.

Since one can define "affordable" only in relation to the total budget, the solution lies not in acquisition reform but in improving the resource-allocation process. Our entire culture focuses on stovepiped portions of resource allocation, producing a system that sometimes encourages self-serving resource-allocation behaviors instead of a cross-functional capabilities approach.

The root cause of this behavior within our process is that we manage by shortfall. Dr. James G. Roche, secretary of the Air Force, said, "Given the demands on the forces, . . . the demands for situational awareness, and a great deal of technology, . . . you can't do the stovepipe game the way you used to."[11] In our current process, we direct the participants to identify their shortfalls and bring them to the table. The result is a process designed to spend more money. Those who are successful in funding their shortfalls are the winners. In addition, since everything we do in the military is very important—life or death issues—cutting back or canceling a program is extremely hard. A process of managing by shortfall provides no information on where we can afford to make those cuts. A lack of information increases the impact of opinions. In other words, personalities fill the vacuum.

Management by shortfall also leads to a tremendously inefficient process for resource allocation. Because individual shortfalls tend to differ each year, the majority of the information needed by the process must be generated anew. Also contributing to this busywork is the fact that the relative priority of the shortfalls changes as well. Adding a 30–50 percent turnover in personnel every year to these conditions has the potential for disaster.

Ultimately, we are trying to determine how much of each capability to invest in relation to maintaining readiness of the forces we have. But how can we do this without knowing the relative value of each capability? All the new business practices coming out of for-profit industry could help the Air Force if it weren't for one detail—we don't make a profit! As Secretary Roche has said, "We recognize this is not a business. We don't have a product, as in the open market."[12] All tough business decisions are based on the relative value of the choices. The new process improvements coming from the commercial sector are designed to help industry leaders find a balance between short-term profitability and sustained health of the business. Without profit as a value measure, the military must develop standards of value to improve resource allocation.

Building a Balanced Program

In August 2000 USAFE began creating its RAM in response to the Air Staff's direction to develop a balanced, capabilities-based input to the Amended POM for FY 03. USAFE's approach entailed dividing the initial top line into groups of capability by assigning each program element to a cross-functional capabilities group. Formation of the groups was based on the relationships between the command's mission-essential tasks and goals, with the scope of responsibility defined by the synergies between the products of these tasks, their relationships to the command's goals, and efforts to minimize the resources that cross group boundaries.

Because USAFE is an operations and maintenance command, management of day-to-day resources drove the definition of capability groups. The command created five groups—information superiority, aerospace operations, logistics support and infrastructure, people, and medical—tasked with assessing the capability provided by each program element and developing a balanced capability within the assigned top line. Each group also had to provide information for USAFE's leadership to balance resources across the groups.

A simple rating system facilitated comparisons among diverse capabilities. Each program-element monitor was tasked to quantify the capability provided by his or her program element. The maximum usable and minimum acceptable capabilities were defined and assigned scores of 1.00 and 0.70, respectively (fig. 1).[13] Each monitor was also tasked to assign a dollar amount to the maximum and minimum capabilities and define what the resources would purchase. Once the scale was established, the monitor was then tasked to assign a capability rating to the initial top line (fig. 2). Although in many cases data were not available to assign a truly objective rating, each program-element monitor had to defend his or her assessment under the scrutiny of peers and to the group.

Although the capability ratings provided a means for portraying the health of each program, they did not form the basis for decision making. Balancing resources within a group or between groups is a process of making trades—taking from one program to help another.

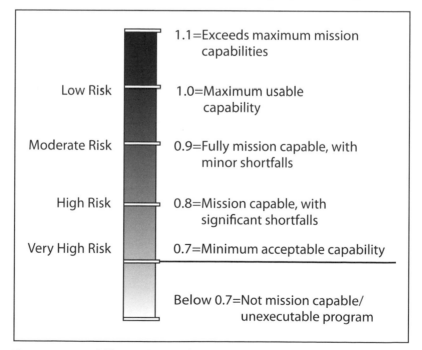

Figure 1. Capability rating scale (Figure courtesy of USAFE/Plans and Programs [XP] office.)

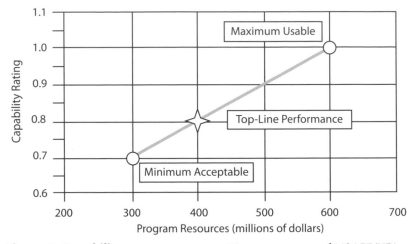

Figure 2. Capability versus resources (Figure courtesy of USAFE/XP.)

To facilitate balancing resources, program-element monitors were tasked to identify trade-ups and trade-offs of capability with the associated resources for their programs. In this way, the group could compare the value of a given trade-up for one program with a trade-off for another and develop an understanding of where the balance lay. Each group identified trades that achieved improved balance across its programs and then prioritized trade-ups and trade-offs for the group as a whole. The groups presented this information to the USAFE leadership, who used it to balance capabilities and resources among the groups. Assuming that the overall command is capable of performing its mission beyond the bare minimum, the goal of making trades was to ensure that each element of capability had enough resources to earn a rating greater than 0.70.

This simple methodology resulted in vastly improved understanding of the capabilities and needs within the command. During the trading process, over $50 million moved among programs to correct imbalances. This amount represented only 2 percent of the command's total resources, but the movement represented 65 percent of those resources within USAFE's control, indicating how unbalanced the program had become without meaningful participation from the major commands.[14] Implementing this process also highlighted several improvements needed within USAFE, along with information the command required from the Air Force to improve the balance further. The command used these lessons to make improvements for the next cycle.

Doing It Again—Only Better

One key to successfully implementing a process change is to include continual process improvement in the design. A good example of preplanned improvement comes from software developers as they actually define processes. In the software industry, the incremental approach for continual improvement is called spiral development, where a spiral includes the development and fielding of operational code.[15] The first spiral might field 60 percent of the desired functions, with succeeding spirals learning from the previous one and fielding increased functionality. In this light, USAFE's RAM for the amended POM of FY 03 is spiral 1, and the command's approach for the POM of FY 04 is spiral 2. The improved RAM/spiral 2 is the result of lessons learned during the FY 03 Amended POM and the desire to tie the model to strategic planning and performance management.

One lesson learned was that managing five groups requires too much manpower from headquarters. In addition, several changes to the group structure were needed to align complementary capabilities, resulting in three groups: command and control, aerospace operations and logistics, and people and infrastructure. The realignment added logistics to aerospace operations, where it is needed most. It also put medical and people together with the infrastructure that supports them and operations.

Another lesson was simply that more time, more training, and a more rigorous process were needed to better implement USAFE's RAM. Following the submission of the amended POM for FY 03, the process was refined, with detailed work sheets provided to the program-element monitors. They were tasked with defining the capabilities and supporting measures for each of their programs during the summer of 2001 in advance of the command's effort to balance resources. These definitions were documented and available for continual improvement during each cycle of the process. In addition, USAFE held a capabilities workshop with Air Force Materiel Command personnel who were involved in performance-based budgeting. The workshop also received support from the Air Force Studies and Analysis Agency, which shared techniques for assessing programs and tying their performance to higher-level capabilities.

A major change implemented for spiral 2 came from aligning the processes for strategic planning and performance management with USAFE's RAM. During a two-day workshop in March 2001, the command's senior leaders created the integrated-management construct for the USAFE Strategic Vision Process (fig. 3), intended to define where USAFE is through performance management, where it wants to go through strategic planning, and how it is going to get there through resource allocation.

The integrated-management construct links the three process elements and ties them directly to resources, links capabilities to resources by defining the command's total mission capability within three capability areas, and then breaks those three capabilities into 14 subelements defined as new mission-essential tasks of the command. Assigning each program element to a mission-essential task aligns all command resources with the capabilities. The construct

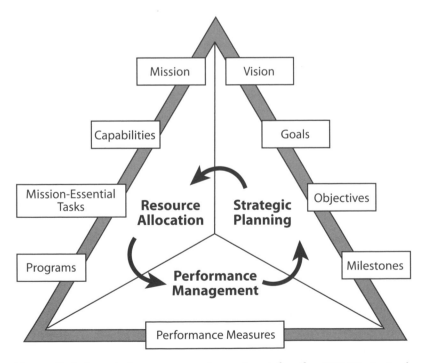

Figure 3. Integrated-management construct for the USAFE strategic vision process (Figure courtesy of USAFE/XP.)

aligns strategic planning and resource allocation by identifying a command goal for each of the three capability areas. One achieves linkage between performance management and resource allocation by aligning the performance measures directly to the mission-essential tasks. The result is a simple framework for aligning strategic planning and performance management with resource allocation.

In addition to aligning resources to take USAFE from where it is to where it wants to go, the new construct will directly improve the resource-allocation process. Dividing the capability groups into 14 mission-essential tasks increases the fidelity for making trades. The new capability groups and their mission-essential tasks used in spiral 2 align the command's 124 program elements (fig. 4). The approach for the FY 04 POM involves balancing the resources within each program element, balancing the program elements assigned to each mission-essential task, and then balancing those tasks within each group. The approach is simple, but experience during spiral 1 proved that establishing capability measures and requirements is challenging. Few programs have useful measures of what is expected from the resources allocated. Comparing the health of each program element

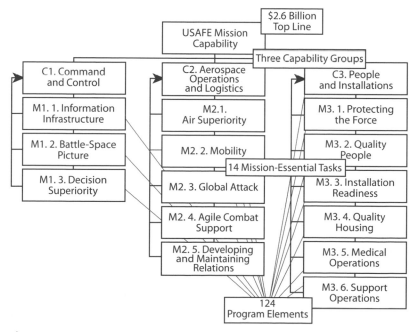

Figure 4. USAFE's RAM (Figure courtesy of USAFE/XP.)

and its contribution to total capability requires measures of that capability that cascade down to the program-element level.

Another significant change during spiral 2 involves integrating the wings' financial and manpower planning into USAFE's RAM. The wings were tasked to create a capabilities-based financial plan for FY 02. The groups reviewed the results of the plan along with manpower assessments to refine their understanding of command capabilities. For FY 03 the wings are using spiral 2 of the RAM to develop an improved capabilities-based financial plan and manpower assessment. Each subsequent spiral will repeat between the wings and command headquarters to develop affordable standards of performance across the command. Those standards will improve USAFE's ability to provide balanced inputs to the Air Force's POM.

The biggest change needed for full implementation of USAFE's RAM will not occur until spiral 3 or beyond and must come from implementation of AFRAP. The required balance among capabilities within the command ultimately depends on having an Air Force definition of the relative value of each capability. As an operations and maintenance command, USAFE receives forces based on higher-level decisions on what capability each weapon system should have, how many systems to purchase, and whether to place them in theater or deploy them from the continental United States. Implicit in these decisions are value judgments based on each system's contribution to national security. An operations and maintenance command has neither the resources nor the information to make such judgments. For this reason, USAFE is working to define what is required from the Air Force to enable the command's resource allocation.

Application to the Air Force

Development of an Air Force RAM is consistent with the direction being taken by AFRAP and would enable the Air Force to balance its resources, based on capabilities. Building an Air Force RAM requires three crucial steps: dividing the resources among capabilities, determining the value of those capabilities, and implementing a process to balance them over time. Dividing our resources in a meaningful way requires development of a planning framework to categorize capabilities. Setting the values for those capabilities demands analysis coupled with continual process improvement, and balancing our capabilities over time requires adding another dimension to the RAM.

Henry Ford taught us that managing anything requires breaking it down into definable pieces. The key lies in making the pieces meaningful and useful for resource allocation. Over the last 20 years, the DOD, the Joint Staff, and the Air Force have developed many excellent planning frameworks. These frameworks were developed for many different purposes but not specifically for resource allocation. Consequently, they don't include all resources, adequately address support functions, or provide distinct categories meaningful to operations. These characteristics are fairly easy to achieve, but none of the existing planning frameworks has them all.

Existing Planning Frameworks

US/DOD/Joint Planning Frameworks

- 13 Title 10 functions
- 2 DOD goals
- 8 tasks in the Universal Joint Task List
- 6 elements in Joint Vision 2020
- 12 areas for the Joint War-Fighting Capabilities Assessment
- 8 areas for the Joint Monthly Readiness Review

Air Force Planning Frameworks

- 3 aspects of the vision
- 6 core competencies
- 7 Air Force tasks
- 14 critical future capabilities
- 6 mission areas in Concepts of Operations (CONOPS) 2020
- 7 elements and 5 capabilities in the strategic concept
- 4 elements in the Expeditionary Aerospace Forces construct
- 7 focus areas in the Vision Force
- 3 Air Force goals

Since the purpose of the framework is to allocate resources, one must include all resources. Existing frameworks for visions or concepts of operations address operational functions, but they leave out the significant peacetime roles assigned by Title 10, *United States Code*. Balancing only a part of the budget will fail to provide the information that decision makers need.

> *The Air Force's core competencies provide an excellent list of the service's unique functions, but the fact that they are unique keeps them from being complete.*

Dividing the whole into manageable pieces is particularly important. Joint and Air Force task lists provide definition for operational tasks but combine all Title 10 functions under a single category. Title 10 breaks "organize, train, and equip" into 13 functions, showing that greater detail is required to describe the roles. However, Title 10 does not address the operational roles of our forces.

Our customers are the joint operations we are tasked to support. Since the customer establishes value, the framework must relate our resources distinctly to operational effects. The Air Force's core competencies provide an excellent list of the service's unique functions, but the fact that they are unique keeps them from being complete. Resources cannot be cleanly divided between precision engagement and global attack. One approach puts weapons under precision engagement and platforms under global attack. But both are usually needed to engage targets, and the operational customer cannot possibly choose between them.

The *Air Force Task List* describes all the activities performed by our service.[16] A thorough review of this list, along with application of the above characteristics, leads to a possible Air Force RAM intended to relate directly to effects-based operations:

- *Global Power* is the key combat capability—the capacity to destroy or disable desired targets.

- *Global Reach* is the capacity to move forces—an enabling capability for engaging targets and a primary capability for humanitarian missions.

- *Global Vigilance* is the capacity to use information—an enabling capability for both reach and power and a primary capability for deterrence.

These three areas encompass the capabilities that directly contribute to operational effects. The proposed RAM also provides coverage of all the Air Force's Title 10 resources in sufficient detail:

- *Agile Combat Support* is the capacity to support forces, whether deployed or not.
- *Quality People* provides a category for all our people programs.
- *Enterprise Management* allows insight into the resources we spend on our immense management task.
- *Innovation and Modernization* group those capabilities used to transform our force and keep it viable into the future.

Each of these four capability areas includes assets that deploy to support operations, along with many used only for Title 10 functions.

All seven of the proposed areas need to have direct costs allocated as much as possible. For example, if hangars are needed for global-attack platforms, the cost of construction and use should be captured under global attack. The costs of acquiring, operating, and maintaining the platforms and associated equipment need to be allocated as well. In addition, manpower and any specialized training attributable to global attack must be accounted for. This is the key to implementing activity-based costing. Secretary Roche said, "We start really hampered by the fact there's not an activity-based costing system."[17] Accounting for costs of the products we deliver is the only way to assess their value.

Once a planning framework is established, the hard part becomes determining the value of the individual capabilities. To do so, one must define the optimum capability measures and associated requirements, which necessitates defining standardized or generic effects applicable to different operational scenarios. For example, we successfully use the ton-miles-per-day unit to help describe our ability to move materiel. Similarly, we need to address the number of meaningful targets per day of power. Then we must do the same for vigilance and the other capability areas. Finally, we must apply these effects to a variety of standardized operational scenarios to determine the driving requirements.

Repeated use of capability measures for allocating resources will result in standards of performance, some of which we can adapt from measures already available, such as combat or "C-ratings" for combat and support systems. We already apply C-ratings to our facilities.

Over time, expectations will be generated for other peacetime services as well. As standards are developed and adjusted, the process of allocating resources will become simpler. These standards will flow directly down to the major command and unit levels through the capabilities framework. The three USAFE capability groups in spiral 2 map onto the proposed Air Force RAM.

The step not yet addressed in USAFE's spiral 2—which must be addressed for Air Force implementation—is addition of the time dimension. Today's modernization-planning process is easily adaptable to AFRAP planning. After developing capability measures and values, one can then establish near-, mid-, and long-term objectives. Current imbalances, the environment, and the affordability of potential solutions will drive these capability objectives. Capability options will be established, and a robust set of options will be funded to ensure a reasonable level of risk.

> *The problem we are dealing with in allocating tens of billions of dollars every year across a nearly infinite series of needs is complex.*

Former Air Force chief of staff Gen Larry D. Welch said, "It's all about balancing modernization, readiness, people, and infrastructure: balancing our readiness today with our readiness tomorrow."[18] Achieving this balance requires implementation of the planning portion of AFRAP. The proposed Air Force RAM enables this implementation by providing the capabilities-based planning framework and the value of those capabilities. Finally, if the Air Force integrates strategic planning, performance management, and resource allocation through a RAM, the result would be a truly "balanced scorecard" approach to management.[19]

Summary and Conclusion

Making the billion dollar decisions that we need to operate efficiently and effectively in the twenty-first century requires three key changes in the way the Air Force does business. The first involves linking resource allocation to performance management and strategic planning. We developed the current processes without a unifying construct. Our experience shows that a management construct relating capabilities to mission-essential tasks and programs provides the needed linkage. The strategic goals align with each capability, and the organizational-performance measures align with each mission-essential task.

The second key change is to create a process that is simple, transparent, and reproducible. The new process must be simple—both to implement and to use. The problem we are dealing with in allocating tens of billions of dollars every year across a nearly infinite series of needs is complex. We can't afford to wait while sophisticated techniques for decision making are developed. We have to get started by tackling the whole budget, not just shortfalls. To do so, we will need to use an approach based on continual improvement. Our current promotion system serves as a good example of a simple process that is subject to continual improvement; it is also transparent and reproducible. As with any new process, it was not as good when first introduced as it is today. Over the years, improvements have made it a highly rated and fair promotion process.

To be successful, a resource-allocation process must also be transparent. Discussing the new DOD management councils for improving business practices, Secretary Roche said, "We are going to be extraordinarily transparent, and so when monies are saved in one area, those monies will then be . . . applied to another area. . . . This is the incentive that is healthy; it's a win-win for everyone."[20]

The process has to reveal the total capability provided by every program and lay the facts on the table for all to see. By defining both the trade-ups and the trade-offs, one can establish the relative value of each choice despite a lack of perfect knowledge. Only then can we agree on what is affordable and reward people for taking cuts for the good of the service.

Reproducibility, the key to the new process's survival, must be based on standards of value that can be established, reused, and improved over time. A single planning framework will help develop the standards, record them as they are established, and clarify the links among programs and their intended operational effects. This framework is actually a categorization scheme. Genghis Khan used a decimal system to manage his armies in groups of 10,000 (called a *tuman*): "Whoever can manage his own house well can also manage an estate, whoever can keep ten men in order in accordance with conditions may be given a thousand and a *tuman* and he will also keep them in order."[21]

The third key change entails developing capability measures that allow Air Force decision makers to deliver the best value to the war fighter over time. General Martin, then a lieutenant general and principal deputy assistant secretary of the Air Force for acquisition, said, "Tying our resources to our capabilities is the single most-important issue facing the Air Force today."[22] We have shown that in order to determine value, capabilities must be related to resources on the one hand and to operational effects on the other. After these relationships are established, we can assess the value of our investments over short-, mid-, and long-term planning horizons. Estimating the value of capabilities and investment options will require analysis, but, in the end, the proposed RAM is a tool for the decision maker—not the analyst.

Our warriors can embrace this particular revolution. It is based on the fundamental principles of establishing teamwork, ensuring capability for the war fighter, and following the money! The improved decision making that results will lead directly to real savings and increased performance by spending the resources where they are most needed. In addition to these direct savings, aligning our efforts will enhance the productivity of the entire Air Force. The biggest obstacle to motivation occurs when people don't know what is expected of them. Sun Tzu said, "He will win whose army is animated by the same spirit throughout all its ranks. . . . But when the army is restless and distrustful, trouble is sure to come."[23] The ultimate improvement in the Air Force will come when our people can be rewarded for providing the war fighter the most "bang for the buck."

Notes

1. USAFE council meeting, Ramstein AB, Germany, 20 April 2001.

2. AFRAP was created in January 2000 under Headquarters Air Force 2002, a major process-reengineering effort led by Lt Gen Joseph H. Wehrle, deputy chief of staff for plans and programs (AF/XP), and guided by William A. Davidson, administrative assistant to the secretary. Maj Gen Danny A. Hogan was the mobilization assistant to AF/XP.

3. Col John A. Warden III, "The Enemy as a System," *Airpower Journal* 9, no. 1 (Spring 1995): 40–55, http://www.airpower.maxwell.af.mil/airchronicles/apj/apj95/spr95_files

/warden.htm; and James A. Kitfield, "Another Look at the Air War That Was," *Air Force Magazine* 82, no. 10 (October 1999), http://www.afa.org/magazine/1099eaker.html.

4. DOD Directive 7045.14, *The Planning, Programming, and Budgeting System*, 22 May 1984.

5. Joint Publication 5-0, *Doctrine for Planning Joint Operations*, 13 April 1995, I-1.

6. Chairman of the Joint Chiefs of Staff Instruction 3100.01A, *Joint Strategic Planning System*, 1 September 1999, E-5.

7. *Government Performance and Results Act of 1993*, Public Law 103-62, 103rd Cong., 1st sess. (17 March 1993).

8. Vice President Gore's National Partnership for Reinventing Government website, 2 October 2001, http://govinfo.library.unt.edu/npr/default.html.

9. The AFRAP process design consisted of four key subprocesses: determine capability objectives, develop capability options, allocate resources, and assess performance. The entire process was to be supported by end-to-end analysis.

10. Office of the Secretary of Defense (Acquisition and Technology), to Secretaries of the Military Departments, memorandum, subject: Reducing Life Cycle Costs for New and Fielded Systems, 4 December 1995, attachment 2, Cost as an Independent Variable (CAIV) working group paper.

11. DOD news briefing, Deputy Secretary of Defense Paul Wolfowitz and service secretaries, 18 June 2001, http://www.defenselink.mil/news/Jun2001/t06182001_t618dsda.html.

12. Ibid.

13. Any scale could have been used, including green-yellow-red or A-B-C. However, allocation of resources favors a numerical system because the next step calls for relating the capability rating to dollars.

14. Dollars moved internally totaled $52 million. Total USAFE resources for the Amended Program Objective Memorandum of FY 03 were $2.6 billion. A $76 million trade space was calculated by subtracting the estimated discretionary funds required for minimum acceptable performance ($1,376 million) from the top-line discretionary funding ($1,452 million).

15. George Wilkie, *Object-Oriented Software Engineering: The Professional Developer's Guide* (Reading, MA: Addison-Wesley Publishing Co., 1993), 111.

16. Air Force Doctrine Document 1-1, *Air Force Task List*, 12 August 1998.

17. DOD news briefing.

18. Meeting, Headquarters USAFE, Ramstein AB, Germany, 2 July 2001.

19. Robert S. Kaplan and David P. Norton, *The Balanced Scorecard: Translating Strategy into Action* (Boston, MA: Harvard Business School Press, 1996).

20. DOD news briefing.

21. H. G. Wells, *The Outline of History* (Garden City, NY: Garden City Publishing Co., 1925), 61; and Valentin A. Riasanovsky, *Fundamental Principles of Mongol Law* (Bloomington: Indiana University, 1965), 200.

22. Tiger Team meeting, subject: Future Modernization Priorities and Process, Arlington, VA, September 1999.

23. Sun-Tzu, *The Art of War: The Oldest Military Treatise in the World*, ed. and trans. Lionel Giles, (Harrisburg, PA: Military Service Publishing Co., 1944), 33.

Contributors

Maj Gen Stephen R. Lorenz (USAFA; MPA, University of Northern Colorado) is deputy assistant secretary for budget, Office of the Assistant Secretary of the Air Force for Financial Management and Comptroller, Headquarters US Air Force, Washington, DC. He previously served as director of plans and programs, Headquarters US Air Forces in Europe, Ramstein AB, Germany. A command pilot with 3,300 hours in eight aircraft, he has served as a staff officer at two major commands, the Air Staff, and the Joint Staff, as well as having commanded an air-refueling squadron and a geographically separated operations group. The general has commanded three wings—an air-refueling wing, an air-mobility wing, and a training wing at the Air Force Academy, where he was also the commandant of cadets. General Lorenz is a graduate of Squadron Officer School, Air Command and Staff College, Air War College, and National War College.

Lt Col James A. Hubert (BS, Oregon State University; MS, George Washington University) is chief of the Strategy and Programming Branch, Headquarters US Air Forces in Europe, Ramstein AB, Germany. Recent assignments have included member of the Air Force Resource Allocation Process Reengineering Team, Washington, DC; chief of Acquisition Management Policy and Acquisition Strategic Planning, Washington, DC; electronic-warfare program manager, Wright-Patterson AFB, Ohio; and Air Force technology coordinator for identification of ground forces, Langley AFB, Virginia. The holder of two patents and the author of several technical papers, Colonel Hubert is a graduate of Squadron Officer School and Air Command and Staff College.

Maj Keith H. Maxwell (BS, University of Maine; ME, University of Florida) is senior military advisor to the commander for Rhein-Main Transition, Spangdahlem AB, Germany. Recent assignments have included chief of programs and legislative liaison, Headquarters US Air Forces in Europe, Ramstein AB, Germany; Peace Vector IV construction manager, Sakara AB and Gianaclis AB, Egypt; chief of the Geotechnical Division and assistant professor, US Air Force Academy; and electromagnetic project leader, Phillips Lab, Kirtland AFB, New Mexico. Major Maxwell is a graduate of Squadron Officer School and Air Command and Staff College.

Conclusion: Why Airmen Must Write!

As I wrote in the beginning of this book, there are many books and stories about many great deeds and leadership traits of our fellow Soldiers, Sailors, Marines, and Coast Guardsmen. They do have a longer history, but they also have a higher propensity to write things down. Go to the book store. In the history and biography sections, you will see the great number of books written by the members of our sister services. I enjoy reading and studying them—especially the ones on leadership.

Airmen also have great stories to tell. We just need to take the time to write them down. As an example, I recently attended the memorial service and funeral of Capt Ryan Preston Hall. He was a 2004 ROTC graduate of the Citadel who, along with three other Airmen, was killed in an aircraft accident in Africa. Ryan's father graduated from the Air Force Academy in 1970 and had served as an Air Force officer.

As I stood watching his mother receive the American flag, she slowly brought her hand up to her mouth as if to muffle a faint cry of sadness. As the ceremony ended, the father came to attention and, standing there in a dark business suit, saluted the coffin that contained the remains of his beloved son.

After his squadron mates honored Ryan with a flyover, I noticed the sea of Airmen dressed in blue that were there to honor their fallen comrade. In the crowd of several hundred, there were at least 100 captains and enlisted Airmen who stood at attention. They all had two things in common: they were all young and all combat veterans. Their youth and the many rows of ribbons on their uniforms reminded me that fighting wars is primarily a young person's business.

These young American Airmen—along with their fellow Soldiers, Sailors, Marines, and Coast Guardsmen—are being served up hard balls by their political and military leaders and are hitting home runs time and again. They make me proud.

As the years pass, their great deeds and the leadership they have demonstrated must not be forgotten. There is an old saying, "We stand on the shoulders of giants." Future generations need the wisdom and the leadership experiences of those who have served before them.

Another old saying is, "A wise man learns from the mistakes of others; a fool has to learn from his own mistakes." Each of us has a responsibility to pass on to others what we have learned over the years. We have a responsibility to mentor those that come behind us. Please take the time to mentor and make a difference. Every one of us is a leader in one way or another.

GPO U.S. GOVERNMENT PRINTING OFFICE: 2012—525-304